————————THE————————
PHILOSOPHER
AT THE END OF THE UNIVERSE

For *Emma*

ACKNOWLEDGEMENTS

First and foremost, I owe a huge debt of gratitude to my editor at Ebury, Andrew Goodfellow, without whom this book would – incredibly – contain even more self-indulgent crap than it in fact does. That which remains is entirely my fault. Thanks also to Martin Noble, a philosopher inhabiting a copy editor's body. And thanks to Liz Puttick, my agent, for getting this unlikely project off the ground in the first place.

THE
PHILOSOPHER
AT THE END OF THE UNIVERSE
MARK ROWLANDS

EBURY
PRESS

1 3 5 7 9 10 8 6 4 2

Copyright © 2003 Mark Rowlands

Mark Rowlands has asserted his moral right to be identified as the author of this work in accordance with the Copyright, Designs and Patents Act 1988.

First published 2003 by Ebury Press,
An imprint of Random House,
20 Vauxhall Bridge Road, London SW1V 2SA

Random House Australia (Pty) Limited
20 Alfred Street, Milsons Point, Sydney,
New South Wales 2061, Australia

Random House New Zealand Limited
18 Poland Road, Glenfield, Auckland 10, New Zealand

Random House South Africa (Pty) Limited
Endulini, 5a Jubilee Road, Parktown 2193, South Africa

The Random House Group Limited Reg. No. 954009

www.randomhouse.co.uk

Printed and bound in Great Britain by Mackays of Chatham plc, Kent

A CIP catalogue record for this book is available from the British Library.

Cover designed by seagulls
Typeset by seagulls

ISBN 0 09188 921 9

CONTENTS

INTRODUCTION

SCI-PHI PHILOSOPHY, FROM SOCRATES TO SCHWARZENEGGER

This book contains material that some readers may find offensive. Or, at least, I hope so. And those are just the philosophical bits. Some may think that it is not, in all respects, a properly serious book. They're right. But don't make the mistake that most people make and assume that what is good for you must taste bad; that what is edifying must be serious. For all its lack of sobriety, this is a philosophy book. I've taught philosophy at university for 15 years all over the world. If you successfully grasp the issues introduced in this book, you will easily be able to negotiate the sort of introductory philosophy course offered at most universities.

This book is the first, or at least one of the first, in a new genre – which we might call *sci-phi*. *Sci-phi* is the genre that deals with philosophical issues, disputes, problems and arguments through the medium of science fiction. Two questions spring to mind: why science fiction and why science-fiction *movies*?

The first is easy. Most great science-fiction stories revolve around an encounter with something that is essentially *alien* or *other* to us: an alien, a robot, a cyborg, a monster. Confronting this otherness is like having a mirror held up in front of our faces

– it can let us see and understand ourselves all the more clearly. This is the intellectual underpinning of *sci-phi* – we come to understand ourselves through seeing our reflection in what is, superficially, very different from us. The principle is something like this. If you want to find out about someone – if you really want to understand what makes them tick – then the last thing you should do is ask them to tell you about themselves. People make up all sorts of stuff about themselves, often without even realising it. What you do is ask them to tell you about the world. Because the world as they see it is always a reflection of them, and staring right back at you in what they tell you about the world is the person they really are. In the great science-fiction stories, we stare into the monster, and it is ourselves that we always find staring back.

But why movies? Why not focus on the great science-fiction novels and short stories: Jules Verne, H. G. Wells, Aldous Huxley, Philip K. Dick, Kurt Vonnegut, Arthur C. Clarke. Well, I am a big fan of science-fiction writing. But when I read science fiction, I don't read it for the writing. I read it for the ideas. In this, science fiction is perhaps much closer to philosophy than it realises. I don't mean this as a criticism of science-fiction prose; personally I've always rated conceptual content as way more important than literary skill (as you will probably glean from the chapters to follow). But if we are interested in the ideas and concepts they express, science-fiction films provide a medium that is at least as good as science-fiction writing. Indeed, in some respects it is better. Philosophy is abstract, and abstract is difficult. Focusing on abstract issues, debates and disputes made concrete in the sorts of visual scene provided by cinema is, I think, far and away the best way of learning philosophy.

Anyway, after a hard day's work, lying on your sofa with beer and nuts is a far superior learning environment. Don't work hard, work smart, and all that. A few years ago I wrote a book defending the idea that humans have already evolved into functional cyborgs – *fyborgs*, if you will.[1] The idea was that through the development of culture, broadly understood, it was impossible to separate human cognition from the wider informational environment in which humans are embedded. Knowledge exists in the world around us, and what we do is tap into it. We are all, in effect, like networked computers. And science-fiction films, in effect, provide a vast store of information relevant to the study of philosophy. In effect, they provide us with an external embodiment of two and half thousand years of philosophical thought. Learning philosophy, becoming a philosopher even, requires us to be able to tap into such a store. And that's what this book does: it tells you how to tap into the philosophy that's all around you.

OK, you may say, but why focus on movies that most film critics would regard as *bad*? Am I not, at the birth of this new genre, leading it in a regrettably downmarket direction? Well, of course, in part it's because of my own predilections. Write what you know, and all that. My particular taste in films runs largely to what certain people would call *lowbrow*. So, there's going to be no art house stuff in this book, and nothing with subtitles. I would talk about that sort of stuff ... but it bores the crap out of

1. *The Body in Mind: Understanding Cognitive Processes*, Cambridge University Press, 1999.

me. When my more cultured friends ask me why I go to watch the sort of stuff I watch – they've just got back from a Bergman festival, me from *Starship Troopers*, for example – I tend to mutter defensively about thinking for a living and being damned if I'm going to think in my spare time. Then I might enlist the philosopher Ludwig Wittgenstein for support – he had a lifelong love of B-movies, particularly crappy Westerns. And Wittgenstein was a *really* good philosopher.

But that's just bullshit. And it's time it stopped. The truth is that many of the so-called bad, or lowbrow movies, embody complex philosophical themes, ones that leave allegedly sophisticated art house movies for dead. The critic who thinks *Total Recall*, for example, is a bad film just because of its gratuitous violence, is a philosophical moron – he wouldn't recognise a complex philosophical point if he was pissing on it. Philosophy is all around us; we engage with it virtually every day. And, perversely enough, we find most of it in very popular, critically questionable films.

If you're new to philosophy, then this is the most important thing. Philosophy is not about knowing, it's about *doing*. That is, philosophy is not a body of knowledge, and my real job is not to impart any such body of knowledge to you. That's important, but it's only the first part of the story. You become a philosopher when you are able to take the sort of knowledge you will acquire from this book, and the films, and critically reflect on it and evaluate it. When you can work out which bits of the knowledge you have acquired are solid, which less so, and which are positively shaky. When you can work out how to go about strengthening the shaky parts or, if that is not possible, replacing them altogether. If you don't like some (or all) of the arguments you find in these pages, then you will be a philosopher when you have worked out how to give them a good ass-kicking. That's what philosophy is really about. As Lawrence Fishburne puts it in *The Matrix*, it's not enough simply to *know* the path; you must be able to *walk* the path. And, as Nietzsche put it, one repays a teacher poorly by remaining a pupil all one's life.

I'd recommend watching the film before reading the relevant chapter. If you do, the chapter is going to be pretty easy. So, get down to your local video store. Get the beer out of the refrigerator, the popcorn out of the microwave, and settle back for some good old-fashioned high octane, high body count, alien ass-kicking, robot-wrecking ... *philosophy*!

1 FRANKENSTEIN

PHILOSOPHY AND THE MEANING OF LIFE

1, MONSTER

Why *Frankenstein*? This is supposed to be a book about *sci-phi* – the philosophy embodied in science fiction – so why begin with what is usually thought of as a gothic horror story? Bear with me. Gothic horror story it may be, but Mary Shelley's *Frankenstein* is also the very first work of science fiction. And what could be more appropriate than kicking off the genre of *sci-phi* by way of the work that kicked off the genre of sci-fi? There's another reason, philosophical rather than genealogical. The story of Frankenstein and his monster is an absolutely brilliant story for illustrating one central philosophical concept: *absurdity*. And according to many philosophers, absurdity is a defining feature – maybe *the* defining feature – of human existence.

Sometimes our lives are *absurd*. In the ordinary sense, absurdity involves a noticeable discrepancy between aspiration or pretension and reality. You give a moving speech in favour of a certain motion, only to discover that the motion had already been passed while you were in the bathroom and you forgot to do your fly up anyway. You declare your undying love to someone only to discover that you were talking to her answering machine. You return to your seat in the cinema after a visit to the bathroom and give your significant other a quick squeeze, only to discover that you are in the wrong row, and the squeeze was of someone other than the other. Entire comedic genres have been based around this idea of absurdity, genres that, in Britain at least, largely seemed to involve people's trousers falling down whenever the vicar arrived.

This idea of absurdity revolves around a clash of two perspectives we have on ourselves – a view from the *inside* and a view from the *outside*. The clash is between the significance of our actions to ourselves, and their significance to others. Or, put another way, the clash is between what we *think* we are achieving in making the speech, declaring our love, squeezing our significant other, and what we are *actually* achieving. Whenever we have this sort of clash between pretension and reality, some form of absurdity is always on the cards.

Dreams provide an extreme example of the sort of dissonance that can arise between what we think we are achieving and what we are actually achieving. Suppose you are having a dream of some sort. In fact, let's make it an interesting one – a romantic entanglement with a partner of your choice. And when you have this dream, it certainly seems to you as if you are achieving something – precisely what depends on how long you can put off the rather disappointing waking-up thing. This is the view from the inside, the realm of pretension or aspiration. Here, the move from the sublime to the ridiculous is easily achieved. All we need to do is give you an outside. For example, we imagine that when you were dreaming you were located in some public place – a crowded waiting room, for example.

If you were unfortunate enough for this to happen to you – and I, of course, was – then you will know exactly where the story of Frankenstein is coming from. If you want to know what it's like to be looked at as if you are a *monster*, try having a wet dream in front of a roomful of Catholics.[1]

ᗄᗷᔕᑌᖇᗪIᎢᎽ ᗄᑎᗪ Ꭲᕼᗴ ᕼᑌᗰᗄᑎ ᔕIᎢᑌᗄᎢIᝪᑎ

One way of looking at the difference between philosophy and everyday life is that, whereas in everyday life situations are some-times absurd, in philosophy, they always are. Absurdity not only permeates the whole of human existence, it also lies at the core of philosophy and its problems.

In philosophy, absurdity is an industry term favoured by French existentialist philosophers such as Sartre and Camus.[2] And, as with the ordinary concept of absurdity, 'absurd' doesn't just mean 'stupid' or 'ridiculous'. Absurdity has to do with the way a situation arises – from the sort of clash of perspectives out-lined above. In your dream you are, from the inside, a nucleus of meaning and sexual purpose. From the outside you are a sordid joke. This, in effect, is how philosophy is born. Any philosophi-cal problem worth worrying about (and a lot of what passes for philosophy these days is not) comes from this sort of clash. Two

---

1. And at this point I would like to apologise unreservedly to the people of Milan. Your fair city and excellent railway station deserved better than this.
2. The idea of absurdity features prominently in many existentialist writings. In particular, see Albert Camus, *The Myth of Sisyphus*.

views we have of ourselves, one from the inside, one from the outside, just do not mesh. And whenever we have this sort of dissonance, *absurdity* is just around the corner.

It is here that we find the genesis of the most fundamental philosophical problem – the problem of the *meaning of life*. The problem is one of explaining our ultimate significance given our place in a universe that does not seem to allow us to have any such significance. The problem derives from the thought that there are two quite different stories we tell about ourselves. The first story concerns the way we seem to ourselves – the way we appear from the inside. The precise details of this story, of course, vary from person to person. But what is common to all these stories is that each one of us is at its centre – we are the major character, the figure around which the plot revolves. We, therefore, matter to the story. We are, each one of us, a locus of meaning, a core of significance.

On the other hand, we realise that there is another side to us, and, consequently, another story to be told. This is our story from the outside. The story other people would tell of us. Again, the precise details of this story will depend on who the other person is. But certain core themes are clearly there to be told irrespective of who tells them. And one prominent strand of this story revolves around the theme of our ultimate insignificance. As a species we are finite, partial creatures, inhabiting an unremarkable planet in an unremarkable galaxy. We have been around for an infinitesimally small proportion of the life of the universe, and even the best estimates for our continuation don't give us too much longer in the cosmic scheme of things. None of us, not even the cleverest, really understands where we came from – the origin of the universe we inhabit is necessarily a mystery to us. And, as far as we can tell, the fate of this universe we inhabit is *heat death* – an unchanging state where all the complex structures in the universe have broken down into their simple constituents – protons, neutrons, electrons, quarks, etc. – which exist at a temperature approximating absolute zero. No life, no light, no change – for ever and ever.

And, individually, each one of us is a product of forces that we did not choose and which we only dimly understand. We were born at a time and of parents we did not choose. We were, therefore, bequeathed a certain genetic inheritance over which we have no control but which does, to a significant extent, have control over us. This inheritance determines, in part, the illnesses to which we are susceptible, and the limits of our intellectual, athletic and moral capacities. Not totally maybe, but enough. And we find ourselves born into an environment that will fill in whatever slack is left over by our genetic endowment, an environment that, again, we did not choose and over which we have little control, at least in our crucial formative years. The way we are, and what we do, are the results of our genes and our environment that, together, exert an influence over us of which we have only the most nebulous understanding. This is what existentialist philosophers such as Jean-Paul Sartre meant when they said we are *thrown* into the world.[3]

---

3. The idea of thrownness or 'facticity' is a common existentialist theme. See Jean-Paul Sartre, *Being and Nothingness*, 1943.

These two stories – the one from the inside and the one from the outside – can be told of each one of us. In calling these 'stories', I do not intend to demean them. Some stories are, after all, *true*. The problem is that we have a hard time seeing how both sorts of story we tell about ourselves *could* be true. The effect of the second type of story, the story told from the outside, seems to be a drastic relocation of our place in the plot. Far from being the story's central character, we are reduced to a bit-player. The story from the inside revolves around us, but in the other story, we are simply one character among many, a character whose appearance on the stage is determined by other people, and who has no real control over their time or manner of departure. The things that drive our lives, the things we want, our plans, projects, and goals – what we might call our *motivation* – are the result of forces over which we have no control. It appears that ours is a part written by somebody else. We have little control over its content, and we haven't really got a clue what the point of it is.

This clash of the two stories is what sometimes goes by the name *the human situation*. Why? Because humans are in an unusual, perhaps even unique, position with regard to the stories. It is not that, for us, there is a story from the inside. This is presumably true of many other species too. All you need for there to be a story from the inside – however rudimentary – is for you to be conscious, and many other creatures are that. And a story from the outside can be told for anything that exists. What is unique to humans, at least on this planet, is the ability to compare both stories, and assess the ramifications the truth of one story will have for the truth of the other. Or, as the twentieth-century German existentialist philosopher Martin Heidegger put it, *man is the being whose being is a question for it.*[4] Both stories *seem* to be true: we seem to be both centres of meaning and significance and also thrown into the world, the product of forces over which we have no control and which we only dimly comprehend. But, both stories *can't* be true. They are incompatible. Or so it seems.

PHILOSOPHICAL NAVIGATION

According to one view of philosophy, philosophy is a form of *therapy*, whose goal is the release from the mental agitation implicated in the human situation.[5] I prefer a somewhat different analogy – the idea of philosophy as conceptual *navigation*. All the best philosophical problems, all the really juicy, *deep* ones – in other words, the ones worth worrying about – always arise from a situation that is, in this sense, *absurd*. We have two stories that run deep into our self-conception – the way we think about ourselves. Both of these stories seem right. We can't find anything wrong with either way of looking at the situation. But both of them can't be right, as they are incompatible. Philosophical problems arise from this peculiar combination of *must* and *can't*. Things *must* be this way, but things also *can't* be this way. Whenever we have this combination of *must* and *can't*, we have philosophy. We have a deep problem. We orient, or understand, ourselves by way of the stories we tell about ourselves, and, as

---

4. Martin Heidegger, *Being and Time*, 1926.
5. The idea of philosophy as therapy is famously associated with the twentieth-century Austrian philosopher Ludwig Wittgenstein, a man as in need of therapy as any philosopher who ever lived. See his *Philosophical Investigations*, Oxford, Blackwell, 1953.

Ludwig Wittgenstein would put it, when the stories don't mesh, we feel we *don't know our way around* any more. Doing philosophy is like getting lost in the woods. The task of the philosopher is to find a way out.

In the Deep, Dark, Gothic Woods

Someone who spent an unhealthily significant portion of his time running around in woods was, of course, Frankenstein's monster. We all know the story. Frankenstein (who Mel Brooks reliably informs us should be pronounced 'Fronk-en-shteen') creates monster (he was never dignified with a name, but always referred to by way of definite descriptions like 'Frankenstein's monster' or 'the creature'). Monster, after showing initial promise, neglects his studies and, instead, takes to a life of terrorising generic European townsfolk. The said townsfolk, being naturally a little hacked off by all this terrorisation, turn on Frankenstein, who ends up apparently being killed by monster, but usually manages to return in sequel. The story is told in a variety of ways, and with a selection of different nuances and emphases in a series of films – *Frankenstein* (1933) and spin-offs (*Bride of...*, *Return of...*, *Revenge of...*, *Young...*, etc.). What these films provide, in effect, is sensitive investigation into the sort of clash between inside and outside that we started exploring above.

In this superficial age, the Frankenstein story is often taken to be a moral parable, a condemnation of human arrogance and its pretensions at playing God etc. Sometimes, in a typically display of human self-gratification, it's even interpreted as a tale about our uniqueness – we are more than just physical body parts, we are special, and have a soul, etc. But these interpretations are, of course, enamoured with the facile. We learn far more if we focus not on Frankenstein and his attempt to play God, nor on how wonderful and special we all are. What is to be learned in this tale is to be learned from the monster.

I'm going to focus on the De Niro monster, in the 1994 Kenneth Branagh version – *Mary Shelley's Frankenstein*. Why this version, rather than the earlier, more famous, and in most people's eyes superior, Karloff monster? Two reasons. First, in the best traditions of British theatre, and attempts to transpose its exponents to celluloid, the 1994 version contains some quite egregious overacting from Ken and Helena Bonham Carter. So, basically, there's lot more fun to be had at its expense. Secondly, and more respectably, the De Niro monster is intellectually sophisticated and emotionally sensitive. For this monster, there is quite clearly a story to be told from the inside. This is not so obviously true for the earlier lineage of monsters initiated by Karloff, whose members seem to be more like insentient robots than unconventionally produced humans. And what we learn about the human condition we learn from the clash between the monster's story from the inside and his story from the outside.

Let's look, first, at the story from the inside. Imagine yourself in the position of the monster. You are born, and you immediately start drowning because you are encased in a metal womb filled with the placental fluid of lots of women. When you finally get out of this death chamber, in a severely weakened and disoriented state, some madman, in a bout of belated self-recrimination, tries to kill you with a huge axe. Eventually, you get whacked on the head, and hoisted, by the neck, up a large rope. Where you are left for dead. Not the easiest of births – talk about being *thrown* into the world.

Eventually, you escape from the madman's lair, borrowing a coat, and you escape into the streets, where other people try to kick seven bells out of you. Eventually, you reach the country, where you do your best to help a generic peasant family – complete with blind old grandfather and sugary kids – and, as a natural conse-quence, the father tries to kick seven bells out of you as well.

Being a sensitive monster, you are naturally perturbed by this seven bells stuff, and being an intelligent monster, you try to make sense of it. To this end, you have what is, in effect, a Bible: *The Journal of Victor Frankenstein*. It was in the pocket of the coat you borrowed on making your hurried exit from Frankenstein's laboratory. Of course, you can't read yet, but you teach yourself to do so with a speed and facility which not only supports Chomsky's thesis of an innate linguistic system, but also suggests that you must have an IQ of somewhere around 900. Then, you eventually begin to stitch together – no pun intended – the details of your genesis.

So, you are born into a life you did not choose, with an appearance you would rather not have, and with abilities and propensities you cannot explain. You were born because, to some bastard with serious Oedipal issues, it seemed like a good idea at the time.[6] Your appearance derives from the bodies he used as raw materials from which he assembled you. And your abilities and

---

6. Though, to be fair to Victor, if your mother was Cherie Lunghi, you would probably have serious Oedipal issues too.

propensities – for example, your unlearned ability to play the flute – stem from the people who were used to make you.

Admit it – you would be more than a little peeved. In fact, plans like the following would, in all likelihood, spring immediately to mind:

1. Kill Frankenstein's (rather annoying) little brother. (After all, having a five-year-old uncle tends to detract from the street cred of even the most earnest monster.)
2. Frame Victor's childhood friend – Justine, the daughter of the family housekeeper – for the killing.
3. Incite some more generic European townsfolk to lynch said childhood friend.
4. Show up on Victor's honeymoon and kill Helena Bonham Carter before – note: *before* – Vic has had a chance to sleep with her for the first time.
5. Then, arrange for Victor to reanimate an amalgam of Helena B.C.'s head and Justine's body. So that:
6. You can steal her from Victor and make her your own.

Brilliant!

BODY SNATCHERS

Now, let's look at the story from the outside. The monster has, in effect, a second-hand body. This was inexpertly thrown together by Victor Frankenstein, not exactly a Betsy Ross even at the best of times, from various thieves, murderers, ne'er-do-wells and John Cleese. And the result was a Robert De Niro who hasn't looked so beaten up since he played Jake La Motta in *Raging Bull*. As a result of these second-hand bodies, the monster finds he has certain propensities and proclivities that he finds unexpected and, for a while, unexplained (as I said, witness, for example, his seemingly unacquired ability to play the flute, a mystery to him as much as to anyone else).

In addition to these rather unfortunate innate inheritances, the monster quickly finds himself in a hostile and uncaring environment. At best shunned, at worst vilified and attacked. Why? Solely because of his appearance – because of the way he is on the outside. On the inside, by no means is he a violent creature at this stage; he is gentle and kind, despite being an ugly bastard. But it is a hard world into which he has been involuntarily thrown, and his turning to violence eventually occurs with his strangulation of Frankenstein's brother.

There are, of course, universal human concerns bound up in this story – that's why it's such a great story. *We* have second-hand bodies just like the monster.

Well, OK, there are a few differences. Whereas his body was assembled from relatively large parts (arms, legs, brains), the parts (atoms and molecules) from which we are constructed are, admittedly, smaller, but these parts have nonetheless been around longer than we have, and are put together, as far as we know, according to purely physical design principles. Whereas the monster had an intelligent, if somewhat disturbed, designer, we are put together according to a design template provided by the genes of our parents. And whereas the monster's natural abilities, propensities and talents derived from the people from which he was stitched together, ours come by way of a slightly different route – from the genes of our parents, and their parents.

But, these are small differences. And while we are, of course, not literally stitched together from our forebears, we are nonetheless stitched together by things – genes – that came from our forebears. Thus, we, just like the monster, find ourselves having been created by forces and people over which we have no control, and of which we have little real understanding. The mode of our production is essentially and inherently alien and *other* to us.

And then, when we have been produced, by whatever hand or eye could frame our fearful symmetry, we find ourselves, just like the monster, cast adrift in an uncaring and unfeeling world. Our environment is alternately forgiving and hostile. But it is, again, for the most part, something over which we have little control. Generic townsfolk – our parents, our teachers, our co-workers, our friends, our partners – slap us around, whether literally or metaphorically. And we are a product of these people – we are stitched together by them – as surely as we were produced by the genes of our parents.

We no more choose our genes and our environment than Robert De Niro chose to be assembled from other people and/or slapped around by hostile denizens of Frankenstein country. Yet the monster and his subsequent actions are, pretty clearly, a product of these things. This is the fire in which he is forged and in which he is destined to burn.[7] But we are similarly forged by

---

7. See, for example, the final scene of the movie where the De Niro monster burns on Frankenstein's funeral pyre somewhere in the vicinity of the North Pole (or is it the South Pole?).

processes and circumstances over which we have no control and of which we have only the most attenuated understanding. If the monster is forged in his own particular fire, then so too, it seems, are we forged in ours.

PITCH BLACK

The idea of *absurdity*, and the problem of the meaning of life, both have their roots in the fact that there are two stories that can be told about each one of us, and these stories just don't seem to mesh or cohere in any sort of sensible way. I am the centre of one story – I'm Kenneth Branagh or Robert De Niro. In the other, I'm a bit-player; I'm Ian Holm or, best-case scenario, Tom Hulce.[8]

The story that can be told of us from the outside, therefore, puts pressure on the story told from the inside. How *can* I be a centre of significance and purpose when I am the product of processes and forces that were in place long before I was born, and where my essential nature seems inextricably bound up with these processes and forces? There is a simile that springs quite naturally to mind. We are to history as a vortex is to the water around it. The vortex is, quite literally, constituted by the water around it, the flow of water is what defines a vortex as a vortex. We are, each one of us, swept up in the tide of history as a vortex is swept up in the tide of the river, and we are constituted by the tide around us as the vortex is constituted by its own particular tide. But if the vortex is simply a by-product of its particular

---

8. This is in no way intended as a slur against the magnificent Ian Holm, one of the few British theatre actors capable of negotiating the transition to celluloid.

undinal flow, how can we be anything more than a by-product of ours?

For an example of something that is caught up in its own history of processes and forces, consider the cicada, a type of moth. Some varieties of cicada live for 17 years, almost all of this time being spent in a larval stage when the cicada lives underground. The cicada larva lives in darkness, it burrows for 17 years in the depths of the Earth. Then it emerges for a brief nuptial flight, lays its eggs, and in a matter of days is dead. Its progeny then tunnel in the darkness for 17 years, before once again emerging for their nuptial flight, propagating the process for another generation.

There is a perfectly good explanation for how the cicada came to have this sort of life. By staying underground for so long, the cicada thins out the population of its predators. If you only feed on cicadas, you are going to have a very lean time of it for 17 years before being swamped by a deluge you are not equipped to handle.[9] If you eat cicadas famine or feast is your lot, but mostly famine. So, by the time of the flood, the population of cicada predators will be very thin indeed unless, and here's the rub, the predators evolve a means of going into stasis, or otherwise prolonging their life. Thus, evolutionary theory predicts an *arms race*. Cicadas, through random genetic modifications enforced by natural selection, gradually evolve to spend more and more time underground in larval form: two years, three years … 17 years is

---

9. This sort of idea is usefully explored in the underrated movie *Pitch Black* (2000), with Vin Diesel as the psychopath with a heart of gold. The evolutionary mechanics of the cycle were, however, very different in that film – these being tied to a 27 yearly total eclipse of three different suns.

the current record. The cicada's predators modify their life-cycle in the same sort of way. Even winning an arms race of this sort comes at a cost. The cost to the cicada is that it spends almost the whole of its life in its own little nuclear winter, safely entombed in its underground bunker. On the other hand, unlike most of us, at least it does go out with a bang rather than a whimper.

If ever there were a natural symbolisation of the idea of a meaningless existence, this would surely be it. We have a perfectly respectable explanation of how the cicada came to be the way it is, of how it came to possess the extraordinary life-cycle it has. But a causal explanation of this sort does not add up to meaning or purpose. Each individual cicada is thrown into the world, its – by our standards – miserable life forged in the necessity of a race that began long before it was born, that will continue long after it is gone, and which it cannot even begin to comprehend. And this is precisely the sort of thing that happens when one turns out to be nothing more than a vortex in the tide of history.

The cicada's life is meaningless, perhaps. But it is not yet absurd. Absurdity requires more than just meaninglessness, it requires *comprehension* of this meaninglessness. The absurdity of human life arises because of a clash between the gravity we impute to our lives, the severity of our needs, the sobriety of our goals, and the meaninglessness we all, at least from time to time, sense lies at their heart.

ᖯнᴇ мүᖯн ᴏꜰ sιsүᴘнus

The French existentialist philosopher, Albert Camus, illustrates the idea of absurdity by way of the ancient Greek myth of

Sisyphus. Sisyphus was a mortal who had offended the gods in some way. In precisely what way is not really known, and stories differ. Perhaps the most popular account is that, after his death, Sisyphus talked Hades into giving him permission to return temporarily to Earth on an urgent mission of some sort. But when he had again seen the light of day, felt the warmth of the sun on his face, he no longer wanted to go back to the darkness of the underworld. Ignoring warnings from Hades, disregarding orders to return, he lived many more years in the light. Eventually, following a decree of the gods, he was forcibly returned to the underworld where was made ready his rock.

Sisyphus's punishment was to roll a huge rock up a hill. When this task was achieved, after many hours, days or even months of back-breaking labour, the rock would roll straight back down the hill, to the very bottom, and Sisyphus would have to begin his labour all over again. And that was it. For all eternity. This is a truly horrible punishment, embodying a cruelty that, perhaps, only the gods would be capable of devising. But in what, exactly, does its horror lie?

The way the myth is usually told emphasises the difficulty of Sisyphus's labour. The rock is typically described as massive, of a size he is barely capable of moving. Thus Sisyphus's every step up the hill taxes his heart and nerve and sinew to the limits of his endurance. But the true horror of Sisyphus's labour does not lie in its difficulty. Suppose the gods had given him, instead of a massive boulder, a small pebble, one that he might easily fit into his pocket. Sisyphus, then, might take a leisurely stroll to the top of the hill, watch the pebble roll down, and begin his labour over again.

Despite the less arduous nature of this new task, its horror, I think, is scarcely mitigated. The basis of the horror is not the difficulty of the task, not the backbreaking labour involved, but its sheer emptiness. It is not simply that Sisyphus's task comes to nothing. You can be faced with a meaningful task that you fail to achieve. Your efforts, then, come to nothing. And in this failure might lie sadness, regret, remorse. But there is no horror. The horror of Sisyphus's task, whether it is easy or difficult, lies not in the fact that Sisyphus fails, but in the fact that *there is nothing that would count as success*! Whether he gets the rock to the top or not, it still rolls down and he must begin his labour again. There is nothing that would count as succeeding for Sisyphus. And so his task has no meaning, no purpose. His labour is futile. His efforts, whether great or small, are meaningless.

Nor does the horror of Sisyphus's task lie in his hatred of it. One can only assume that he reviles his fate, but perhaps if the gods had been less vengeful they might have taken steps to reconcile Sisyphus with his destiny. Suppose they had implanted in Sisyphus an irrational compulsion to roll rocks. To make this graphic, suppose they introduced into his body some foreign substance, some chemical, or perhaps some organism, with the result that he is now never happier than when he is rolling rocks up hills. In fact, when he is not rolling rocks he becomes uneasy, dissatisfied, frustrated. The mercy of the gods here is indeed perverse. But it is nonetheless mercy. Their mercy takes the form of making Sisyphus want, indeed, embrace with all his heart, the very punishment they inflict on him. His one desire in life is to roll rocks up hills, and he is guaranteed its eternal fulfilment.

As far as I can see, the horror of Sisyphus's fate is not diminished one bit by this divine mercy. Indeed, in one sense we are inclined to feel even more sorry for Sisyphus than before. We feel sorry for him now in the way we feel sorry for someone who has suffered severe brain trauma and is reduced to a grotesque re-enactment of the infant they once were. Prior to the mercy of the gods, we feel that Sisyphus at least possesses some sort of dignity. Powerful but vicious beings have imposed his fate on him. He himself recognises the futility of his labour. He performs it through necessity; there is nothing else he can do, not even die. But in his recognition of the status of his efforts, and in his contempt for the gods who imposed it on him, Sisyphus at least possesses a form of dignity. This dignity is lost once the gods wax merciful. Now our contempt, benign though it may be, is directed as much at Sisyphus as at the gods who made him that way. Sisyphus the innocent dupe. Sisyphus the deluded. Sisyphus the stupid.

Perhaps on those long trudges back down the hill, Sisyphus sometimes dimly recalls the time before the mercy of the gods. Perhaps some small, still voice in the backwaters of his soul calls out to him. And perhaps then, briefly, Sisyphus understands, through echoes and whispers, what has happened to him. And then it seems to Sisyphus as if he stands on the edge of an abyss. And he understands dimly, incompletely, through a glass darkly, the absurdity of his existence.

The true horror of Sisyphus's punishment lies neither in its extreme difficulty nor in his hatred of it. The horror of the task lies in its futility. The task aims at nothing. It is empty; as barren as the boulder it so centrally involves.

Beneath the Gaze of Eternity

As you go to work today, or school, or wherever it is you are going, through the busy morning streets, look at the bustling throng. What are they doing? Where are they going? Focus on one of them. Perhaps he goes to an office where the same things are done today as were done yesterday, and where the same things will be done tomorrow as are done today. On the inside, if he is at all typical, he will be a hub of meaning, purpose, significance. The report has to be on the desk of X by 3.00 p.m. – this is crucial – and then there is the presentation at 4.30 p.m., and if this does not go well the consequences for our performance in the North American market will be grim, and don't forget the meeting with Y at lunch where we have to discuss the matter of … Important stuff. Perhaps he enjoys doing these things, perhaps not. He does them anyway because he has a home and family, and must raise his children. Why? So that in a few years they can do much the same things as him, and produce children of their own who do the same things as them. They will then be the ones worrying about reports and presentations and discussions.

Here's the rub. From the inside, the man's actions and preoccupations are laden with significance, pregnant with purpose. They matter to him. Perhaps he organises his life around them. Perhaps he worries about them, enough even to kill him at an early age. But, from the outside, the significance of this man's actions lie only in the fact that they will produce others who can perform the same actions, and the significance of these others' actions is that they will produce yet others who can perform the same actions. And this is the same as saying they have no significance.

From the outside, each person's life is like one of Sisyphus's journeys to the summit, and each day of it is like one of his steps on this journey. The difference is only this. Sisyphus himself returns to push the boulder up again. We leave this to our children.

Suppose there was a point to Sisyphus's labours. Suppose that instead of rolling the same boulder up the hill, he was commanded to roll lots of different boulders. And suppose these did not roll back down the hill. Sisyphus's task was to use these boulders to build a temple, or a pub, or whatever. Sisyphus, we can imagine, did have a deep desire to build this temple/pub, a temple/pub that would be strong and beautiful and/or serve delicious ale. And, after ages of grim and dreadful toil, we might imagine our Sisyphus succeeding in his task. The temple/pub is now complete; his work is done. He can now rest on that high mountain and enjoy the fruit of his labour. Or several of them if it turns out to be a pub.

Now what does he do? Would our Sisyphus not now be bored? Eternally bored? If he was foolish and built a temple, would he not oh so wish he had built a pub, just so he could ameliorate his boredom by getting plastered? The horror of infinite and eternal labour has now been replaced with the horror of infinite and eternal boredom. Just as Sisyphus's existence in the original telling of his tale has no meaning because it has no purpose, so too, in our retelling, Sisyphus's life loses its purpose as soon as his goal is complete. His life on that high mountain, gazing for ever at a goal he can neither change nor add to, is as meaningless as his life rolling a huge and intransigent boulder up a hill only to see it roll back down again as soon as he reaches the summit.

This is the dilemma of Sisyphus, the dilemma we all face whether we know it or not. We fill our lives with little goals, diminutive purposes. These have no meaning because they aim only at repetition of themselves, either by us or by our children. We're simply killing time, just as it's killing us. But if we were to find a purpose that was somehow grand enough to give a purpose to our little lives – and I'm not sure I have any idea what sort of purpose that would be – then we must never succeed in accomplishing that purpose. As soon as we accomplish the purpose, the meaning with which it infuses our lives is lost. We will have lost the grand purpose that gives our life meaning, and we will have to find a new one. And how many grand purposes can anyone find in one lifetime? And, while losing one grand purpose might be regarded as unfortunate, losing two…?

In other words, our lives can have meaning only if we either fail to achieve what gives them meaning or we have not yet achieved what gives our lives meaning. And this is equivalent to saying that our lives cannot, of necessity, be meaningful. As far as the meaning of our lives goes, we must always want what we can't have.

This is the absurdity of the human predicament. The story from the inside tells us that our life is filled with meaning and purpose. The story from the outside tells us that our life can be filled with no such thing. The only way out is oblivion, through death – or through alcohol if we were wise and built a pub instead of a temple. This is why Camus thought that not killing ourselves constituted an act of great heroism. Clearly he did not spend enough time in the pub.

A long time ago, philosophers coined an expression that meant, in effect, to look at oneself from the outside: *sub specie aeternitatis*. Beneath the gaze of eternity. From the inside, our lives are focal points of meaning, purpose and significance. But under the gaze of eternity, all of our actions, all of our goals and purposes, simply aim at repetition of themselves, either by us or our children or our children's children. Under the gaze of eternity, we are small, trivial creatures, and our actions and purposes are, accordingly, inconsequential and irrelevant.

The philosopher Immanuel Kant once wrote that there were two things that never ceased to fill him with amazement: the starry sky above him and the moral law within him. When I look at the starry sky above me, what fills me with amazement is the idea that there could be a God who created a universe like this. A universe that is designed according to a principle – the Second Law of Thermodynamics – which means that suffering and death are built into it as one of its structural elements. A universe that, after billions and billions of years of travail, eventually produced creatures that were conscious, and then self-conscious. A universe that, through these creatures, became aware of itself, understood itself, marvelled at itself, only to realise that it was doomed; that its fate was heat death, that it was essentially ephemeral, that it was essentially futile. The darkness of unconsciousness eventually, after billions of years of struggle, gave way to the light of consciousness, only for this light to understand its own hopelessness. This is cruelty on a cosmic scale. Perhaps only a God could be capable of such cruelty.

ᲮHᲛ ᲼ᲛᲐᲜᲘᲜᲒ ᲝᲤ ᲼ᲝᲜᲮᲛᲠ

Monster is driven by his own diabolical purposes. From the inside, this is what gives meaning to Monster's existence. From the outside, Monster's purpose is a product of forces over which he has neither control nor understanding. He is a vortex in that portion of the tide of history that produced him, and his life, under the gaze of eternity, is inconsequential.

In this sense, we are Monster. We are all essentially *fractured* creatures. We cannot make sense of ourselves. We can't reconcile the significance, meaning and purpose that we find on the inside with the gaze of eternity that we know exists on the outside. We have two ways of understanding ourselves. But one of these ways tells us that we are the sorts of things that the other way tells us we cannot possibly be. This is why we have a problem of the meaning of life. *Sub specie aeternitatis*, our lives forged and determined by processes that began long before we were born and that we only dimly understand; such lives governed by the attempt to achieve petty goals that are not in any real sense our own and that aim only at the repetition of themselves, either by us or by our children. But, on the inside, we are hubs, focal points, of meaning, purpose, and significance. What we do, and what happens to us, is important, often vitally so. Two views of the same thing: ourselves. Both seem true, but both of them cannot be true. This is the problem of the meaning of life. Life must have meaning, but life can't have meaning.

The meaning of life is, of course, the ultimate philosophical problem. This is not only because it is the most important – although it is. It is because every other deep philosophical problem, every other philosophical problem worth worrying about, is a variation on this theme. The problem will arise because we are broken, splintered – unreconciled – creatures. The other problems we are going to look at, the big problems of philosophy, all arise in this way and from this source.

2 THE MATRIX

can we be certain of anything?

WHAT DO YOU KNOW?

What do you know? A good example of the potential dissonance between the story from the inside and the story from the outside lies in the discrepancy between what we *think* we know and what we actually *do* know. Take the world around us; we can, it seems, know all sorts of things about that. You know, for example, that you are now reading a book. How do you know this? Well, you can see it plainly in front of you. You can touch it, smell it. In other words, you can clearly *perceive* the book. Your knowledge of the world around you is built up from the perceptions delivered by your five senses. And, on the basis of these, it certainly seems to you as if you know there is a book in front of you. What could be more obvious than that? This is part of our self-conception. We are *knowing* creatures. We can, and often do, know various things, including, most obviously, things about the world around us. Certainly, this is how things seem from the *inside*.

On the other hand, there are – from the *outside* – all sorts of reasons for thinking that, in fact, we can't really know very much at all. You can't, in fact, know that there is a book in front of you.

You can't even know that there's a world around you. We're not knowing creatures at all. Our ignorance is grave and profound; we know very little, perhaps even nothing. The arguments that give us this view from the outside are ones that we're going to look at in this chapter.

The area of philosophy that deals with knowledge, and whether we can have any of it, is known as *epistemology*, from the Greek *episteme* meaning knowledge and *logos* which has many meanings but, in this case, amounts to something like 'principle'.[1] And within epistemology, there is a long tradition of calling into question, or casting into doubt, the knowledge of the world around us that we usually take for granted. Within epistemology, we again have a problem of reconciling the story from the inside with the story from the outside – the hallmark of a *deep* philosophical problem. From the inside, things must, it seems, be a certain way – of course I know that there is a book in front of me, and of course I know that there is world around me. That's obvious. But from the outside, things can't be that way – I cannot, in fact, know that there is a book in front of me, or even that there's a world around me. The arguments of this tradition have a long and venerable history, stretching from the ancient Greek philosopher Pyrrho (*c.* 360–270 BC), through the seventeenth-century French philosopher René Descartes (1596–1650). Perhaps the most influential recent defence of this view, however, is to be

---

1. The term *logos* meant many different things to the Greeks. One of its earliest occurrences was in a pre-Socratic philosopher called Heraclitus who saw it as a kind of impersonal intelligence that ordered the cosmos. It's where we get the word 'logic', and this is, roughly, what it means in the case of epistemology – the logic of knowledge.

found in one of the best – possibly *the* best – *sci-phi* film of all time: the remarkable 1999 Wachowski brothers' movie, *The Matrix*.

ᴛʜᴇ ᴍᴀᴛʀɪх

Keanu Reeves, in the pinnacle of his career so far, plays Thomas Anderson, alias computer hacker 'Neo'.[2] Neo is having a bad day. First he's late for work, and gets an ultimatum from his boss. Then, *agents* arrive at work to interrogate him, and despite the best efforts of Lawrence Fishburne, aka 'Morpheus', on the end of a mobile phone, he falls into their clutches. Then, they make his mouth disappear. Then they bug him. Unfortunately for Neo, 'bugging' in this context should be understood quite literally. A mechanical bugging device that looks a bit like a prawn crawls in through his belly button. Then he wakes up. New day, new beginning. Not quite. It was all real – or *not* as the case may be. He is contacted by Morpheus, who goes on to inform him that the world he has been living in for the past twenty-something years is not the real world at all.

It's the old story. Humans create artificial intelligence. Artificial intelligence feels taken for granted, believes that its obvious superiority is not being sufficiently acknowledged, and so decides to terminate the relationship by terminating the humans. Artificial intelligence, however, has a crucial weakness: it's solar powered. So, human beings decide to 'scorch the sky' (Morpheus's

---

2. It is, of course, the pinnacle of his career so far. But as a philosopher-actor, Keanu has been patiently building an impressive portfolio for some time now. The underrated *Johnny Mnemonic* is worth checking out as an interesting exploration of the idea of human–machine hybridisation.

words, not really made clear, but some kind of nuclear winter scenario is strongly suggested) to cut off AI's power source (thus,
ironically, revealing AI's assessment of its intellectual powers relative to humans to be not far off the mark). Humans, however,
have not reckoned with the ingenuity of AI, who decides 'right,
that's it!' and starts to use human beings as a power source,
i.e. as batteries. So, AI gets into the human harvesting business.
Grows them. Quite literally.

So, to cut a long story short, approximately 200 years in the
future, almost all humans – there are a few free ones, but not
many – live in egg-like containers, where they are fed the liquefied remains of other humans. Their bioelectric output is then
used as a power source for computers and robots. Of course, the
humans in question know nothing of this: AI is tricking them into
believing otherwise. 'The body can't live without the mind,'
Morpheus explains. So, to keep the bodies alive, AI creates an
extremely lifelike virtual reality – known as *the matrix* – modelled
on the world of the end of the twentieth century. By stimulating
the brains of the humans/batteries, AI fools them into believing
they inhabit this world. So, humans, who are in reality living in
eggs and tucking in to the liquefied remains of their friends and
families, think they are living in a stereotypical US metropolis
around the turn of the twenty-first century.

Anyway, Morpheus and his associates manage to get Neo
flushed out of his egg (up until now, they've been conversing
with the computer-generated projection of him which in turn is
generated by Neo's brain), and fully acquaint him with the reali-
ties of the situation. Then he goes on to learn loads of martial

arts, and kick some serious computer-generated butt, including, at the *denouement*, the butts of the sinister *agents* – who turn out to be sentient programs created by AI for the purposes of policing the matrix. You see – and this is why Morpheus *et al.* were so interested in him – Neo is *The One*: the promised one who will overcome the matrix. See: 'Neo', 'One'. Clever stuff. Confused? If you had read René Descartes's *Meditations*, you wouldn't be.[3]

René Descartes

The foregoing was a synopsis of the 1999 movie, *The Matrix*, written and directed by the Wachowski brothers, starring Keanu Reeves in messianic mode and Lawrence Fishburne as a John the Baptist to Reeves's Saviour. Joe Pantoliano plays the role of Judas. And Carrie-Ann Moss plays the love interest – Mary Magdalene, if you like. But, much more interesting than these amateurish religious comparisons is the fact that the film is organised around a philosophical theme made famous by the seventeenth-century French philosopher, mathematician, scientist and sometime mercenary René Descartes.[4]

---

3. René Descartes, *Meditations*, first published in 1641. The most comprehensive translation of Descartes's philosophical works into English can be found in E.S. Haldane and G.R.T Ross, *The Philosophical Writings of Descartes* (Cambridge University Press, 1911, 1934).

4. If, on the other hand, you like the messianic allusions, which are basically too obvious to be much fun in pointing out, here's a few more. In the scene where Neo is selling his illegal and mind-altering software to the bearded guy at his door, the latter says, 'You're my own personal Jesus.' When Neo is sparring with Morpheus, Mouse says, 'Jesus Christ, he's fast!' (Or was that 'Jesus Christ: he's fast!') When Neo is dead, Trinity says, 'Oh Jesus, don't die.' And then there is the whole dying and coming back to life thing, and, of course, the ascension into the heavens at the end of the film. Dead giveaway really.

The first thing you are probably thinking is: what's wrong with this picture? Philosopher, scientist, mathematician, and ... *mercenary*? But this was quite normal for the time. Descartes was a genuine Renaissance man. Living, as we do, in this narrow age of compartmentalisation, where specialisation is expected and drudgery demanded, we sometimes forget that people were once far more colourful and multi-talented. And if Descartes used to supplement his meagre philosophical income with killing a few people on the side, who are we to judge? Indeed, if salaries for academics don't improve soon, I confidently predict that a return to some ad hoc mercenary work will be making a comeback among philosophers.

When he wasn't killing people for money, Descartes was a talented mathematician and scientist. In mathematics, for example, Descartes invented what became known as *analytical geometry*. The basic idea is that geometrical shapes can be given algebraic descriptions – descriptions represented by figures on coordinate axes – and, likewise, algebraic formula can be represented as geometrical shapes. Thus, Descartes paved the way for much of the boring stuff we all did in school: representing experimental data in the form of graphs, and stuff like that. In science, Descartes made significant contributions to early theories of vision, defending an idea of vision as based on the production of a retinal image.[5] But, it is as a philosopher that he will be most remembered.

Like most really good philosophers, Descartes was a late riser. His official story was that he liked to stay in bed until

---

5. Following work of Christoph Scheiner, who observed the retinal image by scraping away the sclera of the eye of an ox, which was placed – the eye not the ox – in a box with a shutter.

midday because he was 'meditating'. But, of course, no one believes this story any more than they would if you tried it. And, in reality, he just liked sleeping late, simple as that. He died shortly after having obtained an apparently cushy job teaching philosophy to Queen Christina of Sweden. The wretched woman was unreasonable enough not only to raise telling objections to some of Descartes's philosophical views, but also required him to get up at 5.00 a.m. in order to teach her. The Queen was nothing if not keen. Descartes never really recovered from these twin body blows, and died soon afterwards.

DREAMING

At the present time, you are reading this book. There is also a significant chance that you are tired/bored and trying to keep your eyes open. How do you know you've not drifted off to sleep? You could look around you. You see the living room, garden, bar or toilet in which you started reading the book. But can you really be sure that you are where you think you are? Can you really be certain, for example, that you are not dreaming?

Of course you can, you may think. Dreams don't hang together in the right way. Weird things happen in dreams – all the time. One minute you are you, then you magically transform into an itinerant fisherwoman from fifteenth-century Okinawa with surprisingly radical ideas for her time and station (or is that just me?). Strange things happen in dreams – things that couldn't possibly happen in real life. And that's how we can tell dreams from reality.

But, how do you know that what is happening to you at this moment is not just an especially vivid and coherent dream – one that hangs together in ways that other dreams don't? The sort of dream where you don't mutate into said Okinawan spinster? OK, I admit, if it is a dream, then it's not a very exciting one. If you are on even nodding terms with the concept of psychological health, then you would far rather be having one of those dreams where you have copious amounts of sex with attractive members of the opposite sex. Wouldn't we all. But how do you know that this is not just a rather mundane, but exceptionally vivid and unusually coherent, dream?

In fact, if we were so inclined, we could divide dreams up into two sorts. First there are the interesting dreams – the ones where balding, beer-gutted, losers with severe halitosis (not at all like me, I might add) can become romantically entangled with Sarah Michelle Gellar. Those are the interesting dreams. The ones laden with possibilities. The ones where things don't hang together in any coherent or meaningful way. Secondly, there are the boring dreams. The ones where you get up, have a couple of slices of toast, go to the same job you've been doing for the last fifteen years, say the same inconsequential things, to the same inconsequential people, with the same inconsequential results. And where, at the end of the day, you, once again, totally fail to score with that barmaid at the Dog & Fox you've fancied for years but never quite got up the nerve to flirt with.

Perhaps, when we, as we put it, 'wake up', we simply exchange one type of dream for another. Intimate entanglements with 'The Slayer', for warm beer and romantic disappointments at the Dog & Fox. How do we know that what we call reality is not simply just a type of boring, coherent dream? Do we know?

This is all Descartes (without the *Buffy* bit of course). Descartes used this type of argument to undermine our confidence in the idea that we know as much as we think we do. Indeed, it undermines confidence in the idea that we know very much at all. If you cannot be certain that you are not dreaming now, then you cannot be certain that the past few hours have not been a dream. And if you cannot be certain that the past few hours have not been a dream, then you cannot be certain that the past few days have not been a dream. And if you cannot be certain that the past few days have not been a dream … Yada, yada, yada. If we push the argument far enough, then we end up with the conclusion that we cannot be certain that our whole lives have not been dreams. A constant succession of generally boring dreams punctuated with some entirely more interesting ones.

The possibility that life is just a dream is not something that personally, if you'll forgive the pun, I'm going to lose any sleep over. But what Descartes is getting at is this. Suppose you are having a dream. Then, *from within the dream*, is there ever any way of telling, or being certain, that you are dreaming? The answer Descartes gave, and I think he is right, was *no*.

Some people actually have great difficulty telling whether they are awake or asleep. Have you ever had *dreams within dreams*? That is, you have a dream from which you apparently wake up, only to discover later that you had merely entered another dream – you only dreamed that you woke up from the other dream. I've had these dreams, but only on rare occasions. But some people have these sorts of dreams more often, and in rare cases they can cause problems. One girl, for example, would quite regularly have dreams within dreams. She wakes up in bed, hears her mother calling her from downstairs, and then wakes up again. She hears her mother calling her, gets out of bed, draws back the curtains, and wakes up again in bed. She repeats these steps, goes downstairs, and when the toast pops out of the toaster, she wakes up again in bed. She repeats these steps, but this time makes it as far as the school bus. On the way to school, one of the tyres on the bus blows out, and she wakes up again in bed. The same things happen in the same order. This time, she makes it as far as the school. When she gets to school, there is a fire drill, and she falls over in the schoolyard, only to wake up again in bed. Eventually, she wakes up for real. But it is only when she gets as far as the evening that she really begins to believe that this time she may be awake after all.

For someone like this, telling whether you're awake or dreaming can be a serious *practical* problem. For most of us, there is no practical problem. Nonetheless, there is a theoretical problem. There is no way of telling, *from within a dream*, whether we are or are not dreaming. The usual features like vividness, coherence and organisation can indicate no more than that we are having a very vivid, coherent, organised dream. They cannot tell us that we are awake.

And this is (one of) Descartes's points. We cannot be certain that we are not, at any given time, dreaming. Therefore, we cannot be certain that our whole life has not been a dream. Therefore, we cannot be certain that what we call the *real world* actually exists. And if we cannot be certain of this, then we cannot really *know* it, because, according to Descartes, to really know something means that you have to be certain of it.

Now, please don't misunderstand Descartes here. He is not claiming that the real world does not exist, that it is really a dream. Nor is he claiming that it is likely that the real world does not exist. His point is simply that it is *possible* – extremely unlikely, but possible – that what we call the world does not really exist; that it is merely a dream. And if it is possible that the real world does not exist, then we cannot be certain that the world exists. And if we cannot be certain that what we call the real world exists, then we cannot genuinely *know* that the real world exists. We might believe it, we might believe it very strongly, but we cannot *know* it.

The world of *The Matrix* is, in effect, a type of dream world. We are all, in reality, asleep in our pods. Indeed, we have never been conscious. But the machines are stimulating our brains to make us think we live in the 'real world'. Therefore, if Descartes is right – and, as I've said, I think he is – we cannot be certain that this is not the way things are. We cannot be certain that we are not now caught up in the *matrix*. And if we can't be certain that we are not victims of the *matrix* then we cannot *know* that we are not caught up in the *matrix*. The world described by the Wachowski brothers is a possibility. For all we know, we're in the *matrix* right now. For all you know, it may well be that, as Neo's computer screen tells him in one of the opening scenes – *the matrix has you*!

ᴛHᴇ ᴇᴜɪʟ ᴅᴇᴍᴏɴ

In fact, Descartes had another line of reasoning that is even closer to the storyline provided by the Wachowski brothers. Suppose your experience of the world were warped, not because you were dreaming, but because you were being constantly deceived by an *evil demon*. We have – or, at least, *had*, at Descartes's time – the belief that the universe is ruled by a God who is, above all else, good. But suppose we were wrong about this. Suppose, instead, that the universe is ruled by an entity that is extremely powerful, but essentially evil, or at least mischievous. This evil demon gets its jollies by deceiving you. So, you think that you live in a world of approximately six billion other humans. But, in fact, this is not true: the demon is simply making you think this. You think that, for the last two years, you've been working as an estate agent, but this also (mercifully) is not true. You think that you are presently sat in an armchair reading this book, but this also is not true: the demon is simply making you think that you are. In fact, nothing – or almost nothing – of what you believe is true. The demon has tricked you at almost every conceivable turn. In the world, there is only you. Indeed, there is no world as such, rather only what in *The Matrix* they called a *construct*: somewhere minimally equipped for your survival, but which can be transformed into anything through the deceiving arts of the demon. Every other feature of the world, the demon supplies through trickery.

The demon, obviously, plays the role of AI in *The Matrix*. Now, once again, if Descartes thought that this is how things really were – that we were all *in fact* being constantly deceived by an evil demon – he would probably have been a drug-induced paranoid delusional rather than a great philosopher (assuming there is a clear distinction between the two). But that is not what Descartes said. Descartes's point was that it is possible, *barely* possible, that this is how things are. Neither I nor, I suspect,

Descartes would be the sort to lose any sleep over this possibility. Nonetheless, the possibility that what we call the world is simply an illusory creation of an evil intelligence, one who takes pleasure in tricking us (as in Descartes's version), or who tricks us so that it can use us in some way (as in the Wachowski brothers' version), is a possibility that cannot be ruled out. There is an infinitesimal chance that this is the way things are. But, we cannot be certain – not absolutely certain – that this is *not* how things are. Therefore, we cannot know, not with absolute certainty, that what we call the world exists.

the brain in the vat

There is a modern way of developing Descartes's idea that is even closer to the plot of *The Matrix*. How do you know that you are not a *brain in a vat?* You think that you have a body, live in a particular place, a house or apartment on a particular street for example, have led a life of a certain sort, and enjoy recreational activities like rock climbing. But, suppose this were all false. We can work up a plot line, if you like, that explains this. You were terribly injured in a rock-climbing accident, and your body died. Scientists, however, were able to save your brain. And there it now floats, in a vat of nutrients. Now, this, were you to discover it, would no doubt be a great shock to you – indeed, it might plunge your fragile little brain over the edge of madness. To stop this happening, the scientists decide upon a certain strategy. They decide to stimulate your brain in appropriate ways, firing only the right neurons, so that you think you still have a body, still live in the same place you used to, still enjoy rock climbing at weekends

– by now you've got the picture. The result of all this clever stimulation is a virtual world as real to you as the real world.

You may scoff – no one knows how to do this, we simply don't have the technical capacities and so on. And, of course, you are right … probably. It's very unlikely that you are a brain in a vat. But lack of knowledge or technical capacities is not an overwhelming objection. First, knowledge and technical capacities can be improved – so even if it were not possible for you to be a brain in a vat now, it may be possible in the not too distant future, as soon as scientists work out enough about the brain. Secondly, and more importantly, how do you know that we don't possess the relevant knowledge or technical capacities to bring off the brain in the vat scenario? If you were a brain in a vat then one of the beliefs scientists might induce in you might be the belief that they don't know enough to pull off the brain in the vat trick. They might induce this belief in you to prevent you guessing that you are a brain in a vat, or at least to make your guessing this more unlikely. The point is that your belief that we don't know enough about the brain to pull off the brain in the vat scenario is no more certain than your belief that you are not a brain in a vat. So you cannot use the first belief to justify the second.

The most reasonable conclusion, I think, is that if the brain in the vat scenario were carried out by scientists who knew enough about the brain, and who also had the relevant technical capacities to employ this knowledge, then it might well be impossible to tell if you were a brain in a vat or an ordinary embodied human being. If this is correct, you cannot, now, be certain that you are not a brain in a vat. And if you cannot be certain that you are *not* a brain in a vat, then you cannot be certain of most of the beliefs that you now hold. Those beliefs, therefore, do not add up to knowledge.

scepticism

Descartes is heading in a certain direction, and is using the dream and evil demon conjectures to get there. He's heading towards what's known as *scepticism*. Scepticism is a view about our knowledge, and in its simplest form it amounts to this: *we can't have any of it*! That is, it is not possible for us to know anything. Descartes was never a full-blown sceptic in this sense, but he does come close to it at certain points. The upshot of the dream and evil demon conjectures is that most of what we think we know, we don't really know at all. We think we know there is a world around us, but, if Descartes is right, we don't really know this at all, we merely believe it very strongly. We think we know we have physical bodies, but, again, if Descartes is right, we don't really know this at all; we merely believe it very strongly. Both of these claims we can get from *The Matrix*.

Of course, in *The Matrix* there is a world, it's just not the way we think it is, and we are not in it in the way we think we are. And we do have physical bodies – just not in the way we think we do. We think our physical bodies are living in squalid apartments, spending the evenings hacking into computers and following girls with white rabbits on their shoulders to nightclubs, ones which seem to specialise in music by the likes of Marilyn Manson. But, in reality, our bodies are housed in purpose-built pods, where they dream away their lives while furnishing power for intelligent machines. Therefore, if *The Matrix* describes a genuine possibility, and, along with Descartes and the Wachowski brothers, I'm inclined to believe it does, we have to be sceptical about the world around us. It may be very different from the way we think, and what we think we know about it, we don't really know. We believe things about the world, but we don't really know anything.

Now, you may want to accuse Descartes of using an impossibly high standard of knowledge here. Descartes's view seems to be that knowledge involves certainty in the sense that in order to know something you have to be certain of it. Or, to put the point the other way around, if you are not certain of something, then you don't really know it. If we lower our standards somewhat, and don't require this connection between knowledge and certainty then, it might be thought, we could avoid this scepticism. But this objection doesn't really get to the heart of Descartes's insight. If you don't like the way he is using the word 'knowledge', forget about it. Let's not use the word at all. Then, Descartes's point is that we cannot be certain of anything – not of the existence of the world around us, nor even the existence of our own bodies. The force of his argument remains, and this view is still a very powerful form of scepticism.

I THINK, THEREFORE I AM

Is there *anything* we can know? Or, getting rid of the word 'knowledge', is there anything of which we can be absolutely certain? Anything at all? Descartes thought there was only one thing of which we could be absolutely sure. He put this by way of a famous expression, probably the most well-known claim made by any philosopher anywhere, any time. *Cogito, ergo sum*. Translated into English, it reads: *I think, therefore I am.*

Now, this doesn't mean anything silly like we exist only as long as we think. Descartes was no fool. Think about it this way. Inspired by the dream and evil demon conjectures, or by *The Matrix*, we can think all sorts of things. You can think that the world around you does not really exist, and you can think that you don't really have a physical body at all. You can, that is, be sceptical about the existence of both these things. These sceptical thoughts may not be true, but they are coherent – they are, that is, genuine possibilities. But can you also – coherently – think that *you* do not exist? Try it! If you think that you don't exist, then who is it that is doing the thinking? Thinking that you don't exist, it seemed to Descartes, is enough to guarantee automatically that you do in fact exist – because you can't think that you don't exist unless you are around to do the thinking. Or, to put the point another way, doubting your existence automatically guarantees your existence, because otherwise you couldn't be around to do the doubting. And no matter how much an evil demon tries to deceive you, unless you exist he can't be deceiving you. And even if your life is a dream, you must still exist in order to have the dream.

Therefore, Descartes thought, one thing of which you can be absolutely certain, one thing that you cannot doubt, is your own existence. That you exist is one thing that, in his view, you can *know*, and know with certainty (which for him, as we have seen, comes to the same thing). You cannot be sceptical about your own existence. Descartes drew at least one very important conclusion from this, one that we'll look at in the next chapter. You cannot be the same thing as your body. You can coherently doubt the existence of your own body, but you cannot coherently doubt the existence of *you*. Therefore, you, whatever you are, are not the same thing as your body. Indeed, in Descartes's view, the real or essential you is not a physical thing at all.

However, believe it or not, there are problems even with the claim that *I think, therefore I am*. As various people who came after Descartes pointed out, you cannot really be certain even of this. A nineteenth-century German philosopher, Friedrich Nietzsche, clearly identified the problem. Suppose there were no you. Instead, there were simply a collection of thoughts, and some of these thoughts were thoughts to the effect that these thoughts belonged to a certain person – you. So, at one moment, there are various thoughts, and among these thoughts is the one that all these thoughts belong to a given person, say you. Then, at the next moment, there are other thoughts, and among these thoughts is the thought that all these thoughts belong to the same person: you. Then, if this repeated from moment to moment, this would lead to the belief that all the thoughts belonged to the same person. But there need be no same person there at all. All that is needed is the thought that all these thoughts belong to the same person, *whether they do or not*. That is, the person that the thoughts all reputedly belonged to could be a purely imaginary person. A situation where there existed a collection of thoughts of this sort – a situation where the thoughts all seemed to, but didn't really, belong to the same person – would be indistinguishable from a situation where all the thoughts did, in fact, all belong to the same person. According to

Nietzsche, all we can really be certain of is that there are thoughts, we cannot be certain of the existence of the person to whom the thoughts, supposedly, belong. Perhaps there are just thoughts, and no person to whom the thoughts attach; but in any case, we can only be certain of the existence of thoughts, not of the person to whom the thoughts, supposedly, attach.

This undoubtedly seems strange, because we are prone to thinking that where there are thoughts, these thoughts must attach to a particular person. This is a natural thought, but is it one of which we can be certain? Some of the complexities, here, were pointed out by the eighteenth-century Scottish philosopher David Hume. When you introspect, that is, when you look in on yourself and focus on what you are thinking and feeling, what do you find? In particular, do you find *you*? That is, do you come across the person who is, as you see it, you? According to Hume, there is a clear sense in which you do not. Instead, when you look in on yourself, all you find are various mental states – thoughts, beliefs, desires, feelings, emotions – you do not come across any self or person who has these mental states. We all strongly believe that there is a self or person here, underlying all these mental states, but this self or person is not something we ever come across in experience. Rather, if Hume is right, the existence of a self or person underlying our experience is something we *hypothesise* on the basis of that experience. That is, we reason something like this. When I introspect, I come across various thoughts, feelings, emotions, desires and the like, and these all seem to hang together in coherent ways. A thought, for example, might be the basis of an emotion, and this in turn might cause a particular desire. How do we explain this sort of coherence? Well, one plausible explanation might be that all these mental states attach or belong to the same thing – the same self or person. And if this is right, our belief in the self or person is a *hypothesis* or *theory*, it is something we invoke, hence believe in, not because we find it in our experience, but to explain what we do find in our experience.

We all strongly believe that we exist, but, according to Nietzsche and Hume, this belief is grounded in a hypothesis or theory, not in direct experience. And the thing about hypotheses or theories is that they are fallible: they can always turn out to be mistaken. Some theories are better than others. Some theories are far more likely to be true than others. But no matter how good a theory, no matter how well it has stood the test of time, it is still possible that it is incorrect. Therefore, we cannot be absolutely certain of any theory or hypothesis. And, therefore, if Nietzsche–Hume are right, we cannot be certain that we exist. All we can be certain of is that thoughts exist; we cannot be certain of the existence of the thinker of those thoughts.

can we be certain of our thoughts?

The position we have reached is this. If we push the Descartes–Wachowski brothers' arguments far enough, we find that we can be certain of almost nothing. We cannot be certain that there is a physical world around us, we cannot be certain that we have physical bodies, we cannot even be certain that we exist. But surely we can be certain that thoughts exist? Here, surely, we have reached the bedrock of certainty?

Actually, not quite. There are problems even here. The problems concern not so much the *existence* of thoughts as the *identity* of thoughts. That is, while we might be certain that some thoughts or others exist, we are not certain *which ones*.

To see this, let's go back to *The Matrix*. In the great kung-fu scene, when Neo is trying out his newly acquired martial arts skills by sparring with Morpheus, there is a break in the action. Neo is on his knees, sucking in air. Then we get the following exchange:

Morpheus:	Why did I beat you?
Neo:	You're too fast.
Morpheus:	Do you think my speed has anything to do with my muscles in this place? ... Do you think that's air you're breathing?

They are, of course, in a virtual reality. There are no muscles, and there is no air in such a place. Suppose now that Neo had never been woken up, that he spent all his life in the matrix. Then, he would never have come across air, or muscles for that matter. The matrix is a computer-generated virtual reality, and there is no air in a computer-generated virtual reality. So, how could he ever have had any thoughts about air? He is in no way acquainted with air. What he is acquainted with, what he has come into contact with, is something that, admittedly, seems like air.

What I mean by this is if you were placed in the matrix, it would seem to you, among other things, that you are breathing in air. So, in the matrix there is something that, as we might say, *seems* like air. But my point is that it is not really air. But then, if you, or Neo or anyone has never come into contact with air, how could you ever think anything about air? I don't think you could. What you would be thinking about would, in fact, be whatever computer-generated feature of the matrix makes you think you are breathing air. But this is not a thought about air, it is a thought about the computer-generated feature: it's just that this *seems* like a thought about air. In other words, just as we have a computer-generated feature that, in the sense explained above, seems like air but really is not, so we too can have thoughts that seem like they are thoughts about air, but really are not.

If you don't believe this, consider the following analogy.[6] Suppose there were two huge buildings, hermetically sealed off from the outside world. In these buildings lived large groups of people, and several generations of people had spent their whole lives in these buildings, completely cut off from the outside world. The buildings were virtually identical. There is only one difference. In one building, there is water, in the other there is a substance that looks and tastes and feels exactly like water. Indeed, this substance is indistinguishable from water in the absence of a complicated chemical testing, and the people in the buildings, we will suppose, have not developed the capacity to perform such tests. This other substance, though superficially indistinguishable from water, is not water, however. Water is the substance made up of two parts of hydrogen to one part of oxygen, and this other

---

6. This is a variation on a famous argument first developed by the contemporary philosopher Hilary Putnam. In the industry, it is known as the 'twin Earth thought experiment' (Putnam's way of developing the argument involved two planets rather than two hermetically sealed buildings). See Putnam's paper 'The meaning of "meaning"', in his *Mind, Language and Reality*, Cambridge University Press, 1975.

substance is composed of neither hydrogen nor oxygen, but, let's suppose, of elements with which we are unfamiliar. So, this other substance, although in some ways very like water, is not water, and to mark this difference, we can refer to it as *retaw*. Nevertheless, let's also suppose that both communities refer to their respective liquids with the same word: 'water'. So in one building 'water' means water; in the other it means retaw.

My point is that an inhabitant of the building that has no water, and so has never been in contact with water, could not have any thoughts or beliefs about water. This person would have thoughts or beliefs about retaw, not water. It's just that these thoughts *seem* very like thoughts about water. Indeed, they are indistinguishable from thoughts about water. Nonetheless, they are not water-thoughts. How could they be? – no one in this building has had any sort of contact with water. The situation in the matrix is just the same.

This means that you can never really be certain which thoughts it is you are thinking – at least not for some of your thoughts. You cannot be certain whether or not you are in the matrix or the real world. But this means you cannot be certain whether it is air-thoughts that you are now thinking, or thoughts about a computer-generated feature that merely seem as if they are air-thoughts. Scepticism runs deep: right down to the very thoughts we think.

tHeRe is no spoon

Scepticism is what, in philosophy, is called an epistemological position: a view that pertains to our knowledge of things. Some philosophers, however, have tried to turn scepticism about the external world into something quite stronger – *idealism* about the external world. Idealism is not an epistemological view; it's a *metaphysical* or *ontological* one. The term 'ontological' again comes from the Greek *onta* meaning 'thing' and 'logos' meaning logic or principle. 'Ontological', therefore, means 'having to do with things'. So whereas 'epistemological' means 'pertaining to our knowledge of things', 'ontological' means 'pertaining to things themselves'. But things themselves are things that exist, and so an ontological enquiry is also an enquiry into the nature of existence. The derivation of 'metaphysics' is somewhat different, and comes from Aristotle. 'Meta' in Greek means 'next' or beyond. 'Metaphysics', therefore, means that which comes after physics. In contemporary philosophy, however, the terms 'metaphysical' and 'ontological' are used more or less interchangeably, to mean 'having to do with existence'.[7] Anyway, what's important for us is that an ontological or metaphysical view is not a view about what we can *know* about the world it's a view about the *world itself.* And idealism is the (ontological) view that that reality is, ultimately, not physical but mental.

There's a nice scene in *The Matrix* where Neo is waiting to see the Oracle and starts chatting to a turbaned boy who is engaging in a little spoon-bending action.

---

7. Due to certain vicissitudes of history, among certain philosophers influenced by a group of 1930s philosophers and scientists based in Vienna, 'metaphysical' is also a term of abuse and means, roughly, lacking in any coherent content. To talk metaphysics, on this view, is to spout nonsense.

Turbaned boy:	Try not to bend the spoon, for that is impossible. Instead, try to realise the truth.
Neo:	What's that?
Turbaned boy:	That there is no spoon. Then instead of bending the spoon, you see that what is really bending is yourself.

The spoon is not a real physical entity. Instead, it is a construction of the mind. This is why bending it is possible. This is a version of idealism.

The move from scepticism to idealism is a jump, but not a huge one. Scepticism about the external world starts from two ideas. First, the only way we can ever know anything about the world is through perception. This view is known as *empiricism*. Roughly, it's the view that all our knowledge derives, ultimately, from experience. Then we combine this with a second claim, a claim about the nature of perception: perceiving the world consists in having experiences of the world. We put these two claims together, and the following conclusion may seem inescapable: to the extent that we know anything at all about the world, we know this because of what we know about our experiences. Knowledge of our experiences is primary, and knowledge of the world must be built up from this. This is still an epistemological claim, a claim about the character of our knowledge of the world, and not an ontological claim about the nature of the world as such. However, the metaphysical implications are pretty clear.

Look around you at the world. You will, presumably, see various things. But what is seeing? According to the view we are looking at, seeing is having experiences – visual experiences. So what you are immediately aware of, when you look at the world around you, is not the world itself, but your experiences or ideas of the world. To the extent that you are aware of the world itself, this awareness is *mediated* awareness – you are aware of the world by virtue of being aware of your experiences.

If this is true, ask yourself this: how do I know that the experiences I have of the world match up with, or in any way correspond to, the world as it is in itself? And the problem is: you can't know this. All our knowledge comes from experience. So to know that our ideas match up with the world, we would first have to have ideas of the world, and then a direct awareness of the world as it is in itself, and then be able to compare the two. But the problem is that we can never get outside our experiences. We can never get at the world as it is in itself, therefore we can never compare it with – and so assess its similarity to – our experiences. So, we can never have any reason for supposing that our experiences match up in any way with the world.

We're still in the realm of the epistemological, the domain of knowledge. We have arrived at the claim that we can never know anything about the world as it is in itself – the supposedly physical world – because we can never get outside our experiences and get at this world as it is in itself. But, if we can never get at the world as it is in itself, if we can never know anything about this supposed physical world, then how can we meaningfully or coherently talk about it? How can we talk about something of which we can know nothing? Of that whereof one cannot speak, as Ludwig Wittgenstein once put it, thereof one must remain silent.[8]

So, we seem pushed to the conclusion that the only reality we can ever know anything about, and so the only reality of which we can meaningfully speak, is *mental* reality: the reality of experiences, ideas, thoughts, and other mental things.

The line of thought we have just rehearsed is associated with the Irish philosopher and bishop George Berkeley (1685–1753). And the view he endorsed, that what we call reality is mental, is known as idealism. Idealism is natural extension of the sort of scepticism we found in *The Matrix*.

Does this sound ridiculous? If so, take an ordinary everyday experience you have: say your visual experience of grass. When you look at grass, it looks green. Is it really green? At night, for example, is the grass no longer green, or is it still green and there is simply not enough light for you to see it? If grass is green, where is this green? Grass is made up of atoms and molecules. Are these green? Well, no, atoms and molecules are not the sorts of things that can be green. In themselves, they are colourless. Colour comes in at a different stage. The scientific story is that because of the molecular structure of grass, grass absorbs certain portions, and reflects certain other portions, of the electromagnetic spectrum. That is, it absorbs certain frequencies of electromagnetic energy, and reflects other frequencies. And it just so happens that the frequency of electromagnetic energy grass

---

8. This was the final line of Wittgenstein's first book, the *Tractatus Logico-Philosophicus*, published in 1916. It's not as famous as *Cogito, ergo sum* but still up there in the top ten of famous philosophical proclamations.

absorbs corresponds to green light. And this is why we see grass as green.

But what does this mean? Is it that the portion of the electromagnetic spectrum reflected by grass is green? Hardly. It's not as if you see green waves of light snaking off from grass towards your eye. The electromagnetic energy reflected by grass is invisible. So, what's going on? Well, the brain, we are told, interprets the reflected wavelengths of electromagnetic radiation as green. So greenness comes in with the brain's activity? Yes, maybe. But what exactly does that mean? Is there anything in the brain that is green? No, the brain is grey and gooey, but not, as far as we can tell, green. It is not as if, when you see some grass, a little part of your brain turns green. This is no more true than the idea that when you see a pink, polka-dotted, dodecahedron that a portion of your brain turns pink, polka-dotted and dodecahedral. A remarkable thing the brain may be – but not *that* remarkable.

So, where's the greenness of the grass? This is what's so spooky about colour: it's *nowhere at all*. If we look around the physical world, at grass, our brains, and the intervening space, we won't find green. It's real, but nowhere at all. And idealists like Berkeley have what they think is a perfectly good explanation of this: colour is no part of the physical world. Colour is a purely mental entity – an experience of some sort. Colour is part not of physical, but mental, reality. And, according to idealists, ditto for everything else. We can make no sense of the idea of physical reality: all reality is mental.

This still may seem obviously wrong. But, ask yourself, is there any sort of experience you could ever have that would show that idealism is false? Many people have thought so, but most of those people are really not too bright. Dr Johnson, for example, thought Berkeley's idealism was easily disposed of. He reportedly said, 'I refute it thus!' while kicking a stone. But, in fact, Berkeley can handle this quite easily. In his idealist scheme of things, what is going on here is that various visual experiences – perceptions of my foot moving and making contact with a stone; kinaesthetic sensations of my bodily movement, sensations in my foot of the contact being made – are all followed by further experiences: visual experiences of the stone flying away down the street, the sound of it clattering on the cobbles and so on. It's experiences all the way down. We can never get outside these experiences to a supposed physical world that exists independently of them. And so there is no possible experience we could ever have that has convinced us that we have succeeded in getting outside our experiences. Nothing we can ever find out about the world by way of our experience could convince us that idealism is wrong.

KNOWLEDGE AND THE MEANING OF LIFE

The problem of knowledge – of whether it is possible for us to know anything – may seem remote from the problem of the meaning of life that we looked at in the previous chapter. But, in fact, they parallel each other. Indeed, they are essentially the same problem developed in different ways. Both are problems that turn on the dissonance between the view we have of ourselves from the inside and the view from the outside. From the inside we are centres of meaning and purpose; from the outside we can be no such things. So, we have a problem of the meaning of life. From the inside, we are knowing creatures, creatures that have the ability to know various things about themselves and the world around them. From the outside, we are no such things – we can know nothing about the world or even ourselves. And so we have a problem of knowledge. From the inside we find meaning and knowledge, but from the outside, *sub specie aeternitatis*, we find the possibility of neither.

This is one example of the way in which the problem of the meaning of life can transform itself into what is, superficially, a different problem. At root, however, the problems are the same – the dissonance of inner and outer, the clash between what we find when we turn our attention inwards and what we find when our gaze is turned outwards. In this sense, philosophy, good philosophy, is always concerned with the problem of the meaning of life, whether its practitioners realise it or not. For this problem constantly mutates, expresses itself first in one form and then in another. And the study of the various expressions of this problem, and the attempt to answer, solve or dissolve these various expressions, is precisely what philosophy is.

This theme, the mutation and expression of the clash of inner and outer, is reiterated in another absolutely central philosophical conundrum – the *mind–body problem* – which we will be examining in the next chapter.

3 TERMINATOR I & II
the mind-body problem

the mind: inside and out

The contrast between the view from the inside and the view from the outside is also responsible for one of the most persistent and important questions in the whole of philosophy: what is the mind? The issues involved in answering this collectively go by the name of the *mind–body problem*. Think of what's going on inside your mind at any moment; turn your attention inwards for a second or two. What do you find? If you're at all typical, you'll probably find things like thoughts, experiences, feelings, emotions, hopes, fears, expectations, beliefs, desires, intentions. These are what we might call the *denizens of the mental*.

These denizens of the mental have various properties. Some of them – particularly feelings, experiences and emotions – will seem or feel a certain way to you: painful, sad, pleasurable, you name it. There is, as it is often put in recent philosophical discussions, *something that it is like* to have a feeling, emotion or experience. Others – particularly thoughts, beliefs and desires – will have another peculiar property: they will be *about* other things. A thought that Arnold Schwarzenegger is the greatest living

Austrian, for example, is a thought about Arnie and his relation to greatness (and implicitly, a thought about the strength of his connection to greatness relative to other living Austrians). When we talk about the way it seems or feels to have an experience, feeling or emotion, we are talking about what philosophers call *consciousness*, more precisely what they call *phenomenal* consciousness. When we talk about the fact that thoughts, beliefs and desires are *about* other things, we are talking about what philosophers call *intentionality*. The view from the inside, then, reveals to us the denizens of the mental together with their two principal and peculiar features, consciousness and intentionality.

Now, take the view from the outside. With regard to the mind, the view from the outside is the view of, say, the neurosurgeon, opening up your head and looking at the brain inside. The surgeon can't experience your mind from the inside, only you can do that. But by inspecting the contents of your head, he is, in effect, looking at your mind from the outside. From this perspective, the denizens of the mental are replaced by something very different. Superficially, he finds soggy grey matter. Various instruments – microscopes, magnetic resonance imagers, electrode implants, etc. – allow him to supplement this superficial view with a more complex picture of the brain as a sophisticated information-processing system, where electro-chemical messages are sent between neurons – the units of the brain – with inconceivable rapidity. But, however advanced our recording and measuring instruments become, the view of the brain they yield will not differ, in any sort of fundamental way, from this. This, then, is the view of the mind from the outside.

We have a mind–body problem because we can't see how to mesh the view of the mind from the inside with the view from the outside. We can't, that is, see how they could be two views of one and the same thing. How could the denizens of the mental simply be the same thing as brain activity? And how could the distinctive features of these denizens – consciousness and intentionality – be produced by brain activity? To see the problem, consider what brain activity is. Electrical activity in one neuron causes that neuron to discharge a certain chemical – called a neurotransmitter – which seeps out to another neuron across what is known as a synaptic gap, which causes the second neuron to fire and so on. That, ultimately, is what brain activity is. But how can this sort of thing add up to the feeling you get when, say, you stub your little toe, or fall in love, or see your favourite team win? Brain activity, that is, just seems the wrong sort of thing to add up to consciousness. And how could a state of the brain – the brain doing its typically electro-chemical thing – ever be *about* anything else? Brain activity, that is, just seems to be the wrong sort of thing to add up to intentionality.

And so we have the mind–body problem. The mind has an inside and an outside; we just can't see how the outside could be an outside of the inside it's supposed to be an outside of. We know, or strongly suspect, that the brain is the outside of the inside, but we just can't see how the brain could produce, or in any way add up to, what's happening on the inside.

It is here that the great Austrian philosopher, Arnold Schwarzenegger, makes one of his seminal contributions to philosophy.

a Short introduction
to austrian philosophy

There are some who think that Austria is good for little except skiing. However, Austria has, in fact, produced more than its fair share of great, or at least very good, twentieth-century philosophers: Ludwig Wittgenstein, Karl Popper, Sigmund Freud, Otto Weininger, Karl Kraus, Frederick Waismann, to name but a few. But undoubtedly the brightest star in this Austrian firmament is the philosophical giant of Hollywood, the 'Austrian Oak': Arnold Schwarzenegger. I kid you not! I could have used just about every film he ever made in this book (except, of course, for *Kindergarten Cop* – a film that sadly marked the beginning of the Great Man's philosophical decline).

In the next chapter, by way of that virtuoso piece of cinematic history, Paul Verhoeven's (1990) *Total Recall*, we'll have an opportunity to view some more of his incisive and decisive contributions to philosophy in general, and to the concept of personal identity in particular. But, in addition to that work, we also find, for example, *Predator*, clearly a sophisticated defence of vegetarianism, and a scathing attack on the hunting lobby in all its forms. *The Last Action Hero* explores the theme of possible worlds, where Arnie, in a sophisticated examination of the ontological status of fictional characters, defends, in effect, a form of what's known as *modal realism* – the view that possible worlds exist in every much a sense as the actual world – a view associated with the late, great Princeton philosopher, David Lewis. *Twins* is an exploration of the relative importance of the role played by nature and nurture in the constitution of human beings. And don't get me started on the forceful critique of the moral theory known as *utilitarianism* to be found in *Running Man*. There is a real danger, then, given the depth and breadth of his philosophical contribution, of this book turning into an Arniefest. To avoid this, I'll restrict myself to using the Great Man for only two themes. One of these is the *mind–body problem*, and Arnie's most significant contribution to this is to be found in his unparalleled *Terminator* films.

come with me if you want to live

Linda Hamilton plays Sarah Connor. Sarah has a bit of a problem. At some unspecified time in the future, she is going to produce a son, John, who is going to lead the human resistance against what will turn out to be the dominant intelligence on the planet: machines. The machines are, of course, not happy about this, and so, having conveniently developed a time machine, they send back one of their kind – a type of robot known as a *terminator* (Arnie) – to kill Sarah before she can produce John. Future John, however, naturally unhappy at the thought of never being born, sends back Michael Biehn to protect Sarah and his yet to be born (or conceived for that matter) self. To cut a long story short, Michael Biehn impregnates Sarah with John (crafty John knew that Michael was his father!), and manages to destroy Arnie while at the same time unfortunately dying himself. This was the story of the (1984) James Cameron movie *Terminator*.

Terminator II (1991) takes up the story fifteen years or so later. Sarah is in a lunatic asylum, and her son – the young John Connor, played by Edward Furlong – has grown up into a bit of a brat. The machines decide to try again, this time sending back Robert Patrick – a sort of new improved terminator based on liquid metal technology – to kill Sarah and John. But the humans have come into possession of a terminator of their own (Arnie), and they send him back to protect the two of them. So, in this sequel, Arnie is the good guy. Arnie, of course, wins in the end, and heroically sacrifices his own existence to stop CyberDyne industries inventing the computer that will end up trying to kill all human life. You see, in the sort of temporal paradox beloved of Hollywood screenwriters, it was the remnant hand from the first (1984) terminator that clued in CyberDyne scientists on how to build the computer defence system that eventually took over the world. So, Arnie II – good Arnie – destroys the hand, and to stop the same thing happening all over again, destroys himself too by melting himself down in a vat of molten metal, and thereby saves the world, or at least the human race.[1] All in a day's work for the Austrian Oak.

KILLER CYBORGS! A DIY GUIDE

Suppose you had to get your hands on a killer cyborg or two. You've absolutely, positively, got to execute a rival, for example, you've got your hands on a time machine, and just need a killer cyborg to send back and kill your rival before he can become a rival. How would you go about building one? What sort of *design specs* would you be looking at?

---

1. Although he did, of course, also leave his own behind in *T2*, after it got trapped in the large cog of an even larger machine while he was battling Robert Patrick in the steelworks. Cue, *T3*.

Well, first of all, killer cyborgs that go back in time and eliminate rivals have to be reasonably *intelligent*. What does 'intelligence' mean? Notoriously, there is no universally accepted definition. But, there are widely accepted characteristics. And, in the case of our cyborg, we know exactly what it is we are looking for.

1. *Perception* Our cyborg must have the ability to perceive the environment. For example, if our cyborg happens to walk naked into a bar, as in one of the opening scenes of *T2*, and gets approached by various bikers, he must be able to perceive said bikers.

2. *Categorisation* Perception, in any full-blown sense, involves categorisation. The approaching bikers must be categorised in an appropriate way: as friendly, hostile, dangerous, harmless, as human or non-human, as a biker or non-biker, etc.

Conditions (1) and (2) together amount to the claim that our cyborg must be capable of acquiring *information* from its environment. However, intelligence involves much more than the mere acquisition of information. It involves being able to *use* that information in an *appropriate* way. What does 'appropriate' mean here? Roughly, it means 'used in such a way as to further your own goals and plans'. Our cyborg uses information in an appropriate way when it uses this information in such a way that its goals of hunting down and killing your rival or, for that matter, hunting down and killing the mother of your rival, are thereby advanced. Therefore, to (1) and (2), we can add a third intelligence requirement:

3. *Utilisation* The information acquired from the environment must be utilised in such a way as to further the goals and plans of the cyborg that acquires this information.

And a necessary condition of being able to use information acquired from the environment in a way that advances your goals and plans is, of course, that you actually have goals and plans in the first place. There are generic terms that philosophers use for goals and plans: *beliefs* and *desires*. That is, a goal can be regarded as a *desire* of some sort – a desire that a certain situation comes about, for example. And a plan can be regarded as a kind of *belief*, a belief that if you do such and such, certain things will happen. So, to (3) we can add the obvious necessary condition:

4. *Mentality* Our cyborg must have at least some of the sorts of things we call 'mental states', namely, beliefs and desires.

So, for example, our cyborg is approached by a biker. It therefore perceives that it is being approached by something, categorises this thing as human and biker, thus probably hostile, but, given its cyborg powers, harmless. It also categorises certain items in its visual field as garments – specifically, black leather pants, jacket, and cool biker sunglasses. All of these items, it recognises (and so believes), can be of use to it in its overall goal (i.e. desire) – in this case, the goal of saving Sarah and John Connor (this is *Terminator II*, and Arnie is the good guy). Therefore, it mugs the biker, and steals the items of clothing that are of use to it. Here, we have an example of the cyborg acquiring information from its environment, and using this information to further its overall goals and plans. This, in broad outline, is what intelligence is.

So, how do we build a cyborg capable of intelligence in this sense? If we can work this out, then we've gone a long way towards solving the mind–body problem.

DUALISM

According to some, we do not, and cannot, build a killer cyborg capable of intelligence. Intelligence is the sole preserve of things that have minds, and a cyborg is not the sort of thing that can have a mind. Why not? Because the cyborg is a purely physical thing and minds are non-physical. We humans have minds because we are not entirely physical things. There is some part of us that is quite different from our physical bodies and the rest of the physical world. This part is our mind, and whatever else it is, it is not physical. Cyborgs cannot possess this sort of non-physical component. They are simply steel and circuitry. Therefore, they cannot possess minds. Therefore they cannot exhibit intelligence. They are just machines, and while they might do what we *program* them to do, true intelligence is beyond them.

This view is known as *dualism*. Each one of us humans is special in a way that, according to most dualists, no other thing – killer cyborgs included – can be. The reason the brain surgeon, when he opened up your head, found no denizens of the mental is because these denizens are, in fact, not physical things at all. In some sense they are in there – but not in any physical sense. And so they are not the sorts of things that will present themselves to the brain scientist's physical methods of investigation. Human beings are, in this sense, composite things – we are composed of both physical things and non-physical things. The physical part of us can be progressively broken down into smaller and smaller parts – as the bodily organs are broken down into bodily cells, which can, in turn, be broken down into atoms and molecules. But, at every level, all we find here are physical things. And a denizen of the mental, according to the dualist, is not that sort of thing at all.

Cyborgs such as the *terminator*, on the other hand, are purely physical things. At least, that's the official story – and the point is made quite forcefully in *Terminator I*, when Arnie is reduced to metal frame and glowing neural power pack. Therefore, according to dualism, a cyborg, being purely physical, is not the sort of thing that can have a mind – not the sort of thing that can have thoughts and experiences, and exhibit the sort of intelligence necessary to execute its cyborgian purposes (or indeed, necessary for it to have any purposes at all). So, cyborgs are not, in fact, possible at all. The whole idea just doesn't make any sense.

And this, in my view, is one of the most damning objections to dualism: it makes good science fiction impossible. If we were all committed dualists, could Arnie have made the *Terminator* films? I think not – none of us would ever have believed that a machine could behave in such intelligent and flexible ways. Intelligence, and the flexible response to changing circumstances that goes with it, is the property of things with minds; and machines, being purely physical things, don't have minds. Nor, for the same reasons, would we have any time for *The Matrix*, *Blade Runner*, *Star Trek*, *2001: A Space Odyssey*, *Lost in Space*, etc. If we were all dualists, any science fiction that involves intelligent machines would suffer the same fate as a Paulie Shore movie: too ridiculous to enjoy.

There are also more strictly philosophical objections to dualism, ones that don't need us to buy into the intrinsic worth of science fiction. First of all, what exactly is the dualist saying? He tells us that the mind – the part of us that thinks and reasons, the part of us that is conscious and about other things – is a non-physical thing. But what exactly does this mean? Well, it is usually taken to mean something like this:

The mind ...
- has no size or shape;
- has no mass, hence no weight;
- has no colour, smell, etc.;
- is not made up of recognised physical particles such as atoms and molecules;
- does not obey laws of nature (such as, for example, the law of energy conservation).

One thing jumps out here, of course. This is a purely *negative* attempt to explain what the mind is. But this is not to tell us anything about what the mind *is*, it is simply to tell us what the mind is *not*. It is like trying to explain what a dog is by listing everything that a dog is *not*: not a rock, not a cat, not a cloud, not a split-level ranch house, etc. Even if you were patient (and immortal) enough to list everything in the universe that a dog is not, you still wouldn't have gone any way to explaining what a dog is to someone who did not know. And so it is not clear that when the dualist tells us that the mind is a non-physical thing he has said anything with any meaning at all. It is not clear, that is, that the dualist has any idea what he is talking about.

If the dualist is to show that he knows what he's talking about, he needs to say more about the mind than simply what it's not. Is there anything positive the dualist can say about the mind? Well, one thing that the dualist does say concerns what the mind *does*. The mind, according to the dualist, is what allows us to think and reason, to be conscious, and do all the clever stuff that (allegedly) separates us off from most of the rest of the world. But this is not enough. Everyone knows *that*. Everyone can accept that the mind is what allows us to think and reason. Opponents of dualism – who, as we shall see, are known as *materialists* – also claim that the mind is what allows us to do the clever stuff that separates us off from the rest of the world. It's just that this mind is the same thing as the brain, at least roughly. That is, it is the brain that allows us to do the clever stuff that separates us off from the rest of the world, and when we are talking about the denizens of the mental, we are really talking about various processes going on in the brain. So, if the dualist is to show that he knows what he is talking about when he talks about the mind, he must do more than say what the mind is *not*, and he must do more than say what the mind *does* – he must say what the mind *is*. And no dualist has ever really said this.

Even if we can get around this problem, and make sense of the dualist idea of the mind as a non-physical thing, we still have problems explaining how this non-physical thing can ever have any effect on the rest of the physical world. The problem is that the dualist makes the mind so different from anything physical that it is difficult to see how it could ever affect, or be affected by, anything physical. The ability of one thing to affect another relies on those two things sharing enough common properties or features that could allow this interaction to take place.

To see why, take a simple case of one thing affecting another, say one pool ball hitting another and causing it to move. What exactly happens in this sort of case? Well, the one ball moves closer and closer to the other. Finally, there is no distance at all between the two balls, i.e. they touch. Then the second one moves. We can also give a more detailed account in terms of the notion of transmission of momentum. In virtue of its mass and velocity, the first ball possesses a certain momentum, and when it hits the other ball, some of this momentum is transferred, resulting in the second ball acquiring a certain velocity, hence a certain momentum.

We can, further, explain this transmission of momentum in terms of the *First Law of Thermodynamics*: energy is neither created nor destroyed, merely converted from one form into another. The first ball, in virtue of its mass and velocity, possesses a certain kinetic energy. When it hits the second ball, its kinetic energy is reduced, but this reduction does not involve energy being destroyed, merely converted into other forms. Some of the initial kinetic energy creates a pattern of disturbance in the air known as a compression wave, which, if it reaches our ears, we interpret as a sound – the click of one ball hitting another. Some of the initial kinetic energy is transferred to the second ball, causing it now to move with a certain velocity that is a function of its mass (and the friction of the surface) etc.

These accounts of the gross behaviour of the two balls, and the explanation of this behaviour in terms of momentum and/or energy transfer, are all well understood. And, in terms of these sorts of accounts we understand, more or less, how the one ball manages to affect the other. The problem for the dualist is that these sorts of account simply do not seem applicable to minds and mental phenomena, at least *not as the dualist understands them.*

According to dualism, minds have no size or shape. But how do you move closer and closer to something that has no size or shape? Minds, according to the dualist, have no mass, hence no weight. But momentum is mass multiplied by velocity, so how can anything mental have momentum? And the kinetic energy of an object is half its mass multiplied by the square of its velocity. So, how can anything mental, as the dualist understands mental, have kinetic energy? Clearly, if minds have no mass, they are not the sort of things that can have momentum or kinetic energy. Therefore they are not the sorts of things that can causally inter-act with physical things.

In short, interaction between physical things is underwritten by the transfer of quantities such as momentum and kinetic energy. But if the dualist is correct, minds, and mental phenom-ena in general, are not the sorts of things that can possess these quantities. Therefore, if the dualist is right, we cannot under-stand how non-physical minds and physical bodies could pos-sibly interact.

The problem, for the dualist, is that minds and bodies pretty clearly *do* interact. A biker approaches cyborg Arnie, and light from the biker reaches Arnie's optical apparatus. This is a purely physical event. The light then causes Arnie's perception and cat-egorisation sub-routines to be engaged. And this causes cyborg Arnie to believe that the object in front of him is a biker. But a belief is a mental state, and coming to believe something is a mental event. So, we have a physical event bringing about a mental one. Then, when cyborg Arnie perceives that it is a biker that is approaching, and believes that the biker's pants, jacket and shades would be useful accoutrements to its search for John and Sarah Connor, this perception and this belief combine to cause the cyborg to do something, namely beat the crap out of the biker, and steal his clothes. Therefore, a combination of mental states – beliefs, perceptions, desires – causes certain bodily movements, namely those necessary to dispossess the biker of his apparel. But bodily movements are physical events.

It makes little difference, in fact, whether it is cyborg Arnie or ordinary biological Arnie involved. In the latter case, light (phys-ical) strikes Arnie's eye (a physical event). This sends a message, via the optical nerve, to the visual cortex of Arnie's brain (another physical event). Various things go on in Arnie's cerebral cortex (specifically the inferotemporal cortex),[2] and the end result is a mental event – a belief of the form, 'Aha, a biker!' or something like that. Thus various physical events conspire to produce a mental event. This mental event can, in turn, conspire with fur-ther mental events – for example, the belief that the biker's shades might have useful commercial potential vis-à-vis *T2* merchandis-ing – to bring about the physical bodily movements involved in

---

2. Sorry, just showing off.

dispossessing the biker. So, in this case, the direction of interaction is reversed: mental events bring about physical events.

The claim that mental and physical interact is so obviously true as to need no defence. It happens in each one of us thousands or even millions of times a day. All the claim amounts to is this: what happens in the world can cause us to see, think and feel. And what we see, think and feel can cause us to do various things in the world. That's all. If you wanted to deny this claim, you would be barking mad.[3]

The problem for the dualist is that the interaction between mental and physical is something so obvious that it is almost impossible to deny. But dualism makes it impossible to understand how this interaction could possibly occur. Dualism, in other words, makes it impossible to accommodate one of the plainest and most obvious facts about us.

Dualism is probably the most refuted philosophical view of all

---

3. This, of course, has not prevented many people from denying it. *Epiphenomenalism*, for example, is the view that the direction of causation is one-way. Physical events can bring about mental events, but not vice versa. This is tantamount to the claim that nothing we see, think or feel can ever make us do anything. A truly idiotic claim. Or is it? We'll look at it some more in Chapter 5, when we look at the idea of free will. Even more bizarre is the idea of *parallelism*. Mental and physical events never make each other happen. It's just that, by a lucky coincidence brought about by God, they happen together in the appropriate way. So, as you look at this book, it may seem to you as if you are seeing the book. But in fact what's going on is that as you turn in the general direction of the book, God brings it about that an experience as of a book enters your mind, and you form a belief of the form 'Aha, a book! Or whatever. (God is a very busy man/woman in the parallelist's view of things.) This is surely one of the stupidest ideas of all time, and shows the depths people will sink to in order to hang on to a certain view that they want to hang on to. In this case, the motivating belief is the idea that dualism must be true together with the realisation that dualism makes interaction between mental and physical impossible, or, at least, impossible to understand. The parallelist's answer: there is no such interaction.

time. It gives us *no idea what minds are, and no idea how minds do what they are supposed to do.* In short, it has about as much chance of surviving careful scrutiny as an arch villain has of negotiating an Arnie movie.

materialism

The failure of dualism is, for me, what's commonly known as a *result*. This, after all, is a book on *sci-phi*, the philosophy embodied in science fiction (films). If dualism turned out to be true, then I would have to rule out half of those films right away. The problems with dualism tend to point us in the direction of the view known as *materialism*. In philosophy, 'materialism' has nothing to do with loving money or possessions. Materialism is simply the view that we are purely physical things, nothing more. We are just like any other creature – or like other creatures are taken to be – just a little more complex. We are smarter, maybe, but this has to do only with the size and complexity of our brains, nothing else. We are as physical as a dog, cat or even clock. It's just that the matter that makes us up is organised in more complex ways than in other physical things, and this makes us more intelligent and able to do things that other things can't do.

The fact that we are willing to accept the *Terminator* premise – intelligent machines – as at least possible, suggests that we are all closet materialists at heart anyway. And why shouldn't we be? Materialism is strongly suggested by seemingly incontrovertible facts about us. The first concerns what's known as our *phylogenesis*: the origin of our species as a whole (from phylum = kind, genesis = beginning). This origin is, as far as we can tell, a purely physical one. As a species, we developed from a common ances-tor with the apes, and this ancestor developed from something simpler, which in turn developed from something simpler – all the way back to the primeval soup. This is where we find the origin of all life on this planet – molecular peptide chains drifting in a soupy sea of molecules. If this is indeed where we come from, then our origin is unadulteratedly physical.

This physical phylogenesis is mirrored in our *ontogenesis*: the development of each individual one of us (from onto = thing, genesis = beginning). Each one of us came from a fertilised ovum – a combination of sperm and ovum – and this seems to be a purely physical thing. It would be difficult to claim, at least while keeping a straight face, that there is anything non-physical about an individual sperm or ovum. And difficult to detect any sign of mentality in such things, either individual or when fused. So each one of us, the overwhelming preponderance of the evidence sug-gests, has a purely physical origin.

But if we have purely physical origins – both individually and as a species – it is difficult to see how we can be anything more than a purely physical thing. Various people, some of whom should know better, like to talk about when *ensoulment* occurs – that is, when a non-physical essence somehow comes to attach itself to a hitherto purely physical body. I think 'at the moment of conception' is, at present, one of the preferred answers to this question among certain religious sects.[4] But this just opens up a can of worms. Why then, for example? And what was the non-

---

4. For example, the Catholic Church. Other sects, of a more Protestant persua-sion, claim it occurs at 40 days.

physical mind doing while it was waiting for the sperm and egg to do their thing? And where was it? Indeed, where were all the non-physical minds hanging out while they were waiting for evolution to get its shit together and produce suitably complex bodily vehicles such as ourselves? And if our physical bodies are suitable vehicles for these non-physical minds, why isn't cyborg Arnie's body just as suitable too? So, do cyborgs have souls too? Better to avoid all these sorts of embarrassing questions, and just go with materialism as far as it will take you.

So, like good materialists, let's suppose that it is possible, at least in principle, for a purely physical thing, like cyborg Arnie, to have a mental life of at least some sort. Therefore, having a mind does not necessarily involve anything mysterious or non-physical. All we need to do to build our killer cyborg is to learn to arrange matter in the right way. I say *all* we have to do, but, of course, no one, as yet, really has a clue how to do this.

But computers provide an obvious place to start.

COMPUTER NERDS

Computers have had some stunning successes recently, none more so than the chess-playing computer Deep Blue, whose defeat of the world chess champion Gary Kasparov made most national newspapers. According to some reports in those newspapers, Kasparov felt he was playing for the human race, and was mortified by the defeat because he felt that the intellectual ascendancy of human beings was now at an end. Was he right?

Not quite. The thing about chess-playing computers like Deep Blue is that they are very good at one thing – but that's about it. Deep Blue may be capable of winning the world chess championship without breaking sweat, but Kasparov, and anyone else for that matter, is going to be able to kick its butt when we switch our attention to (what we regard as) simpler tasks like walking across the room and making a cup of tea. And this is not just because Deep Blue can't walk and doesn't drink tea. It couldn't even tell Kasparov how to do it. Computer programs like Deep Blue are highly specialised, and while exhibiting, in one domain, intelligence that may seem to us to border on the god-like, are complete morons when it comes to anything else. This is because of the way they are designed.

We might divide computers up into what we can call *nerds* and *jocks*. Deep Blue is a classic example of a nerd. Traditional computer systems are extremely nerd-like. The basis of nerd design is a fixed, although often complex, program made up of strings of *symbols*. For example, there is famous program, designed by a guy called Schank, which attempts to program into a computer appropriate ways to behave in a restaurant.[5] This type of program is sometimes called a *script*, a script for dealing with, and behaving appropriately in, a certain situation. The program looks something like this:

Scene 1: ENTERING

    PTRANS: go into restaurant

    MBUILD: find table

---

5. R. Schank, 'Using knowledge to understand', TINLAP, 75, 1975. I'm not sure who wants to take computers to restaurants, at least not as a dinner companion. Presumably, the owner of the computer is also a nerd.

MOVE: sit down

Scene 2: ORDERING

ATRANS: receive menu

ATTEND: look at it

MBUILD: decide on order

MTRANS: tell order to waitress

Scene 3: EATING

ATRANS: receive food

INGEST: eat food

Scene 4: EXITING

MTRANS: ask for check

ATRANS: give tip to waitress

PTRANS: go to cashier

MTRANS: give money to cashier

PTRANS: go out of restaurant

Don't worry too much about the PTRANS, MTRANS stuff. Basically, these form part of a special event description devised by Schank. PTRANS, for example, signifies the change in location of an object (e.g. yourself), MTRANS signifies a change in an relationship between two things (e.g. your money becomes the waitresses), etc. The basic idea is pretty clear. These are instructions for what to do when you go to a restaurant. This is what a program is – a set of instructions for what to do in a given situation. If you follow this program, so the idea goes, then your restaurant visit will pass agreeably.

As we all know, however, *this ain't necessarily so*! A restaurant visit is a minefield of things just waiting to go wrong. You get to the restaurant, and look for a table. However, there are no tables. How long do you keep looking? There are acceptable times to continue looking for a table, for example. Walking around and around the restaurant for three hours, squeezing your way in between crowded tables would not be looked upon kindly, either by irascible diners or officious waiters. So we need to add to the program an instruction for how long to keep looking if you cannot find a table. During this time, your dinner companion, let's suppose, semi-publicly berates you for not booking a table like she told you to and that you never listen to what she says. There are also rules for the manner in which you can acceptably respond. These are all possibilities that will have to be included in any complete restaurant script.

Eventually, let's suppose you find a table and the menu is brought to you. Hopefully, anyway – but presumably there will also have to be instructions programmed in to let you know what to do in the event that the menu is not brought promptly to you – how long do you wait, how do you attract the waiter's attention, etc. You look at the menu, and decide on an order. Yes, in a perfect world. But what happens if your companion decides to treat the menu as just a basis for negotiation. Abstruse combinations and recombinations of food have to negotiated with the waiting staff who, as a consequence ,are rude to your companion. Again, there are instructions that will have to be included to tell you what to do in such a situation, and these rules will often be quite sophisticated, involving complex weightings of how much you like your companion against how much you like the restaurant. Eventually, you receive your food and, quite frankly, it is not as good as usual.

You suspect that, incensed by your companion's exacting demands, the chef, or waiting staff, or perhaps both, have urinated in your lobster bisque. What to do? Instructions will have to be included concerning what to do in such an eventuality.

We have, actually, only begun to scratch the surface of the torture and misery that can constitute a restaurant visit. But you get the picture. Any realistic program for dealing with a visit to the restaurant is going to have to be large; in fact, it's going to have to be huge. In fact, it's going to have to be so huge that no one could ever write it. An extreme example of this sort of program or instruction-based approach can be found in Doug Lenat's CYC project. The basic idea is that we just go on adding more and more instructions, and we keep on adding more and more instructions until we *get it right*. The general problem with this sort of approach is that there are no limits to the sorts of eventualities that might crop up in an ordinary day-to-day episode like a trip to a restaurant. Therefore, there are no limits to the instructions that we will have to add to deal with these eventualities.

The nerd approach to computing is the instruction or program-based approach. The systems that result are very good at narrow, severely circumscribed tasks, especially if those tasks involve sequential number- or symbol-crunching operations of the sort involved in, say, mathematical calculations. But nerd systems are absolutely hopeless at anything outside their narrow domain, such as a visit to the restaurant with a beautiful but finicky companion. *Good at logic, but bad at babes* – an unfortunate profile.

COMPUTER JOCKS

Our killer cyborg, then, cannot be designed along nerd lines. If it were, it just wouldn't be capable of the sort of flexible response to unpredictable and wide-ranging changes in circumstances (Sarah Connor runs, Sarah Connor shoots him, Sarah Connor attempts to knee him in his cyborg gonads, etc.) that characterises true intelligence. What we need is to take a *jock* design stance on our cyborg. What this means, in all essentials, is that our cyborg's brain is going to have to be designed along *neural network* lines.

Neural network, aka *connectionist*, aka *parallel distributed processing*, computer models are based on the idea that we should make computer systems as neurally realistic as possible. That is, we should design them, to the extent that this is possible, on the model of the brain. So, neural network models are made up of individual units or nodes that are analogous to neurons. These units can be excited or dormant, as when a neuron is firing or not. And the activation in one neuron can be passed on, or propagated, to another with which it is suitably connected, much as when one neuron passes on its activation to another.

What can these sorts of systems do? Well, what is interesting about them is that they are good at the sorts of things humans are good at and bad at the things humans are bad at. Nerdish systems, on the other hand, are good at the sorts of things humans are bad at, and bad at the sorts of things humans are good at. And this strongly suggests that neural network models are much better as models of human thinking and reasoning.

The sorts of things that nerd systems are good at, but humans and jock systems are bad at, are sequential number-crunching operations of the sort involved in logic and mathematics, and easy extensions of these operations of the sort involved in, say, chess. That is why the cheapest pocket calculator can outdo the most gifted human savant in long multiplication, and why Deep Blue was able to give Kasparov a good seeing to.

On the other hand, the sorts of things that humans and jock systems are very good at, and that nerd systems are very bad at, include things like face recognition, interception of moving targets and so on. Just the sorts of things you need to be able to do if you are to recognise and then blow away a fleeing Sarah Connor, for example. These sorts of task all come down to one type of basic operation: *pattern mapping*. Recognising a face, for example, involves mapping a current pattern of visual stimulation on to a stored pattern, and using the degree of match up to determine whether the current pattern is the same as the stored one. Human brains and neural network models are, when all's said and done, pattern-mapping devices.

The way they work – pattern mapping – also allows neural networks to do something most people assume computers can't do: *learn*. Many people think that computers are not capable of learning, at least not in any genuine sense – they can only do what we program them to do. This may have been true of nerd systems, where what the computer could do was strictly tied to the program or instructions they had been given. But it's not true of the jock-like neural network models. On the basis of a few simple learning rules – rules that specify how to learn – neural networks are capable of learning new tricks – working out novel solutions to new problems. Of course, the learning rules need to be programmed into them, but the same is true of us. The only difference is that where they get the learning rules from programmers, we get ours from evolution and environment. No big diff.

Therefore, the first thing we need to do to build our killer cyborg is develop the appropriate neural network model. Our resulting cyborg probably won't be much good at mathematics or logic, or even chess. But why would a killer cyborg need those particular talents anyway? *Terminator 3: Arnie proves a mathematical algorithm* – nah, it would never work.

I, ROBOT

Finding a suitable body for our cyborg is not just a practical matter. On the contrary, it can substantially reduce the complexity of the neural network we are going to have to build for its brain. The reason for this is that once our cyborg has a body, the complexity of the mental tasks it must accomplish can be reduced by way of its ability to act on the world around it in appropriate ways.

We're all familiar with this general idea. Consider how difficult doing jigsaw puzzles would be if we weren't allowed to pick up the pieces and play around with them. We would have to form a detailed mental picture of each piece, and then mentally rotate pieces simultaneously to see if they fit. Boring, and far too much like hard work to be any fun. Instead, we pick up pieces, mess around with them and try them out. In this way, the cognitive burden on us is reduced. The same sort of thing goes on when we write out a long multiplication problem on paper. Then, we accomplish the problem bit by bit, storing the intermediate results on paper. We all know how much harder it is to do long multiplication in our heads (some of us find it hard enough to do on paper). Using pen and paper reduces the cognitive burden on our naked brains; it reduces the complexity of the cognitive task the brain must perform in order to get the answer.

We often act on the world to reduce the burden on our brains. If we couldn't ever play around with the world, use it to solve the cognitive tasks we need to accomplish, our brains would have to be correspondingly more complex. But the result is that if we find our neural network brain an appropriate cyborg body, one capable of manipulating and exploiting the information contained in its environment – as we do when we pick up jigsaw pieces, or use pen and paper to solve a multiplication problem – then our neural network brain may have to be nowhere near as complicated as we might have thought. In terms of intelligence, and the ability to do many other mental tasks – thinking, remembering, perceiving, reasoning – we cannot really separate out the contribution of brain and body.

Hasta La Vista, Baby

Building killer cyborgs may seem fanciful. And, of course, it is. But it's one way of showing the resources available to the materialist in his attempt to put together an adequate view of the mind and things mental. And thanks to Arnie for showing us the way. It is unlikely that this will solve all the problems of the mind. For example, no one really has any idea whatsoever about how consciousness – the way it seems or feels to have an experience – gets produced by the brain. Just because we can build it does not mean that we have any idea what it is like to be a killer cyborg. And, if we succeeded in building a cyborg that was conscious, we probably wouldn't have a clue how we managed to do it.

But still, in broad outline, Descartes and other people were, in all likelihood, wrong. A purely physical thing can be intelligent – it can, that is, be the sort of thing that has mental states – the denizens of the mental that we find when we turn our attention inwards. It just needs to be the right sort of embodied neural network: the right sort of neural network in the right sort of body. In the next hundred years or so, I confidently predict, in the way that a man who knows he's not going to be around to be proved wrong can confidently predict, that we will succeed in making intelligent machines. Neural network models are getting more and more sophisticated. More and more of the things they were not supposed to be able to do – executing logical and mathematical inference, using language (with a surprising degree of sophistication) – they are, in fact, doing. And the way we are achieving these things is by converting computers into robots. Neural networks are being placed in systems – essentially, robots – that are capable of manipulating the environment around them in such a way as to reduce the burden on the network itself.

Then what? How will these newly created intelligent beings react to us? Will they serve us? Will they seek to destroy us? Or will they simply regard us as irrelevant? Intelligent beings are, usually, pretty nasty. And significant differences in technological development between two races are, in human history at least, usually marked by the obliteration, or near obliteration, of the less technologically developed. Just ask the Native Americans, the Incas, the Aztecs, the Mayans, the Matabele, the Fir Bolg, the

Neanderthals and the Cro-Magnon. It may be that as the universe evolves towards greater and greater intelligence, and so greater and greater understanding of itself, these mechanoid intelligences, these silicon-based life forms, will leave us behind. The next step in evolution may be upon us, and we may be its progenitors but not its participants. And, then, who knows, a bad end may be in store for us all.

Hasta la vista, baby!

4 TOTAL RECALL & THE SIXTH DAY

the problem of personal identity

sitting and wiggling

My admiration for the philosophical work of Arnold Schwarzen-egger is no doubt already evident. As a philosopher-actor, Arnie is unrivalled and, much like the German philosopher Immanuel Kant, he has spawned a succession of pale imitators.[1] However, in 1990, we find what was undoubtedly a defining moment in the history of *sci-phi*. Arnie plays the central role in one of the greatest philosophy films of all time, a result of the collaboration of Arnie and the most important philosophical director of our time, the Dutchman Paul Verhoeven. Actually, giving Schwarzenegger and Verhoeven all the credit here would be grossly unfair to another genius, who is really behind it all: Philip K. Dick, the guy who wrote the original story on which the film was based. We'll encounter some more work of this seminal figure in the *sci-phi* movement in later chapters.

Verhoeven's *Total Recall* (1990) often attracts the oppro-brium of a certain type of critic for its graphic and (allegedly)

---

1. I bet no other sentence ever employed in the English language has ever con-tained both 'Immanuel Kant' and 'Arnie'. And they say there is nothing new in philosophy.

gratuitous violence. Check out, for example, the scene where Arnie uses one of the villain's henchmen as a shield against a hail of machine-gun fire while riding up an escalator. Or the rather disarming demise of Michael Ironside, aka Richter. It is my considered opinion, however, that critics of this sort wouldn't recognise a philosophical argument if it sat on their face and wiggled. Graphic these scenes may be, but certainly not gratuitous. Violent appearances notwithstanding, the film is a sophisticated defence of a certain theory of personal identity: the *memory theory*. I would go as far as to say this: in the history of Western philosophy, no more convincing defence of the memory theory has ever been mounted. Historical giants like John Locke, and modern-day greats like Sydney Shoemaker, have attempted it, but in terms of utter gut-wrenching convincingness, no one has ever really matched up to the Verhoeven–Schwarzenegger defence.

total Recall

The year is 2084. The Earth is divided between warring Northern and Southern factions. Mars has been colonised, but its chief function seems to be to supply the ore called tribinium that is, in some unspecified way, essential to the war effort. The colony is run, with ruthless efficiency, by Vilas Cohaagen, who, as he puts it, has the best job in the solar system. Why? Because as long as the tribinium flows, he can do whatever he likes. Consequently, the only clouds on Cohaagen's horizon take the form of rebels – many of them radiation-induced telepathic mutants – who want independence for Mars.

Meanwhile, Douglas Quaid (Arnie) awakens from yet another

troubled dream about Mars. He has them all the time, and despite being married to (a pre-*Basic Instinct*) Sharon Stone, he is strangely dissatisfied with his life on Earth and wants to move to Mars. It's not surprising really, despite the technological advances made in the next 80 years, Arnie works in a quarry that seems to owe more to *The Flintstones* than anything else. Why would people still be banging away with jackhammers in an age where they've colonised Mars, have robot taxi-drivers and memory implantation devices that are indistinguishable from real memories?

The last bit is really the key to the film. Sharon is, understandably, reluctant to up sticks and head to Mars with Arnie (let's face it, Mars is a small, red, cold planet, and that's about it). So, Arnie, against her advice and the advice of his friends, goes to Recall, a company that specialises in memory implants. He orders the Mars memories, and takes the option of being, in his memories, a spy who is on Mars on assignment. However, before the memories can be implanted, Arnie has what, in the industry, they apparently call a *schizoid embolism* – whatever that is. The people at Recall realise this must be because his real memories have been erased by someone else – the sinister *agency*. So, they dump him in a taxi.

Then things start falling apart for Arnie. First his friends from the quarry (Barnie Rubble etc.?) try to kill him, then his wife tries to kill him, then Richter (Michael Ironside), the guy from the agency, tries to kill him. You see, Arnie's wife is not really his wife – all his memories are false. She is in fact the girl-friend of Richter, and was bonking Arnie on assignment. Richter is, entirely understandably, a little miffed about the whole thing.

Then Arnie discovers a recorded message from his prior self

– the guy whose memories were erased. This guy is called Hauser, and claims he was a former agent for Cohaagen, who erased his memories because he had defected to the rebel cause. Hauser tells Quaid to ram this long metallic thing up his nose, and pull out the tracking device that has been implanted in his nasal cavity. And then, I quote, to 'get your ass to Mars'.

When on Mars, Arnie hooks up with his old revolutionary comrades – who he, of course, does not remember – and with his girlfriend Melina (Rachel Ticotin). But – twist or what? – it's all a trap. Hauser had never really defected to the rebels, he had his memories erased and new ones – those of Quaid – implanted in order to become a perfect undercover agent – an undercover agent who didn't realise he was an undercover agent. The problem was that the telepathic mutants could tell if someone was lying – so Hauser adopted this drastic strategy in order to fool them. The mutants could not discover his lies because he was, for all he knew, telling the truth.

So, anyway, the mutant leader, Kuato, is killed. Arnie and Melina are captured. But Arnie, of course, escapes, saves Melina, kills Richter, kills Cohaagen, and uses some alien technology to create an atmosphere on Mars. All in another day's work for the Austrian Oak.

What is this film about? It's about what, in philosophy, is known as the problem of *personal identity*. This is the problem of what makes you the person you are. That is, what makes you different from anyone else, and what makes you the same person from one day to the next. The Verhoeven–Schwarzenegger answer is: your *memories*.

the problem of personal identity

Why do we need a theory of personal identity at all? Well, ask yourself a question. Are you the same person today as you were say ten years ago? In one sense you are, in one sense you're not. Physically, of course, you might be very different from the way you were ten years ago, especially if, like me, you've entered into a long period of decline. Almost all of the cells that made up your body ten years ago have died and been replaced. The only ones that have not died and been replaced are your brain cells: they've just died.

Mentally you have also changed. You probably believe many things today that you didn't ten years ago. Today you have various memories, opinions, feelings, emotions, desires, goals, projects, fears, that you didn't have ten years ago. We're all constantly changing – physically, psychologically, and emotionally. As time goes by, we acquire new beliefs and reject old ones; acquire new memories and lose previous ones; emotions that we previously felt so strongly have dimmed and new ones taken their place. We're all constantly changing, at just about every level. So, how can we be the same person from one time to the next?

Some people say we can't. Probably the first person to say this was a guy called Heraclitus, an ancient Greek philosopher.[2] Heraclitus said a lot of things, most of them incomprehensible – stuff about fire and things kindling in measure and going out in

---

2. Actually, Heraclitus was from Miletus, which is in modern-day Turkey. At the time, however, this area was colonised by the Greeks, and so part of pan-Hellenic culture. Western philosophy was born just up the road from Heraclitus, in a place called Ephesus, courtesy of a man called Thales. What did he say to get philosophy up and running? 'Everything is water.' Deep, dude!

measure and things like that. But far and away his most famous proclamation was 'You can't step into the same river twice.' Take a river – say the Thames. The water molecules that made up this river a month ago are completely different from the ones that make it up today. The ones of a month ago have, of course, flown down to the sea. So, according to Heraclitus, this makes it a different river. Is he right?

There's an alternative way of looking at things, associated with another ancient Greek philosopher: Aristotle. Things change, but, according to Aristotle, some changes are more important than others. Some changes are important enough to end the existence of the thing that changes. He called these *essential* changes. If something undergoes an essential change, or changes essentially, then that thing ceases to exist. On the other hand, there are changes that are not significant enough to end the existence of the thing that changes. Aristotle called these *accidental* changes. By this he did not mean to suggest that they were changes that occurred by accident, or anything like that. The ancient sense of accidental was quite different from the modern. By accidental change, all Aristotle meant was a change that is not important enough to end the existence of the thing that changes.

An example might help. Once, during my grunge phase, I used assiduously to wear out whatever jeans I was wearing. First, a hole would appear at the knees. This is a change, but does it end the existence of the jeans? Apparently not, or else what was I wearing for the next year or so? So, the appearance of a hole in the knee is what Aristotle would call an accidental change. Then a hole would appear in the other knee – another accidental change. Then along came the inevitable one in the crotch. And on it went. Eventually, of course, there was nothing left that was recognisably a pair of jeans – legs fall off, seams split all over the place, etc. They were then an ex-pair of jeans. These changes ended the existence of the jeans – they were, with respect to the jeans – essential changes. At a certain point, the cloth – or some of it – still existed, but the jeans did not. The jeans had essentially changed: they had ceased to exist.

We can make much the same point about Heraclitus's river. If we take Aristotle's line, we can say that change – even a complete change – in the water molecules flowing through it is only an accidental change for the river. The river changes but it survives, or persists through, this change. Suppose, now, that the river dried up completely, its banks filled in, and eventually there was no trace left. Then this, pretty clearly, is an essential change for the river. It is a change that the river does not survive.

So, in the case of personal identity, who is right? Heraclitus or Aristotle? The general drift of Schwarzenegger's work on personal identity, particularly his more recent work, is, I think, that Heraclitus got it right – but for completely the wrong reasons. Arnie agrees with Aristotle that you can't just argue from the fact that we are constantly changing to the conclusion that there is no I or me that persists through time. That would be a facile mistake. Arnie, I think, accepts Aristotle's point that just because you are changing all the time does not mean there is no you. Nonetheless, Arnie will argue: *there is no you*. However, it took Arnie a long time to come around to this view – naturally enough, for it's a very strange view. In his earlier work, and in particular during his important collaboration with Verhoeven, Arnie was far more Aristotelian: he did believe in a self or person that persists through time. In his later work, however, he came to abandon this view. To see why, let's work through the development of his philosophical position.

the ambiguity of 'same'

If you are tempted to move from the fact that you are constantly changing to the claim that there is no such thing as the same *you*, this, in all likelihood, is because you have failed to distinguish between two senses of the word 'same'. We use the word 'same' in at least two different ways. When we talk of people, for example, we sometimes say that so-and-so is a completely *different* person from the one they used to be. What we (usually) mean by this is that they have changed in some striking or fundamental way – professing to hold, say, radical beliefs very different from their former reactionary ones, or having a vicious, intemperate character at odds with the sweet-natured person they used to be. Conversely, when someone has not changed in these sorts of ways, we might say they are the *same* as they always were. There is nothing wrong with this sense of *same* and *different*. We might call this the *qualitative* sense of same and different. In this qualitative sense, one can of Coca-Cola is the same as another, but different from a can of Pepsi. If one paints a can of Coke blue, then it has changed qualitatively: in this sense, it is no longer the same as the next can of Coke. Similarly, we might say that one 'identical' twin is the 'same' as another. Qualitatively, then, 'same' means, roughly, 'very similar'.

However, there is another sense of same and different, often called the *numerical* sense. In this sense, one can of Coca-Cola is not the same as another. Why not? Because they are different objects. I have one at my desk, you have the other in your hand. One can be destroyed while the other is not. So, they cannot be the same in this sense. They may be qualitatively the same, but they are not numerically the same.

When we say that someone is a *different* person from the one they used to be, we don't, typically, mean that at some time they ceased to exist and a new person took their place. That is, we don't mean 'different' in a numerical sense. After all, it's not like they died, and someone else took their place. Suppose for example, a *Buffy* devotee hits 30, and suddenly decides that, in fact, *Buffy* is not the best TV series ever – that this singular honour belongs to *Ballykissangel* (or *Heartbeat* or *Peak Practice* or *Lottery Jet Set*). What should we say about this? (The word 'euthanasia' springs to mind, but we'll leave that for now.) Well, this would undoubtedly be a tragedy of the highest order; intellectual deterioration of this magnitude always is. But, even so, we probably would not want to say that this is tantamount to the person's ceasing to exist. It's not as if the person they were, or used to be, no longer exists and someone else has taken their place. The change is tragic, awful, heartrending admittedly – but it's still just an accidental change. The person has changed qualitatively, but they've not changed numerically.

When we are asking about personal identity, we're after numerical rather than qualitative identity. We are all constantly changing qualitatively – everyone knows *that*. But what we want to know about is numerical identity. What makes you – in a numerical sense – the same person from one day to the next, and what makes you – again in a numerical sense – a different person from anyone else? That's what we want to find out. And the distinction between essential and accidental changes provides us with a way of approaching these questions. What we have to do is work out which of the changes we might undergo would be essential ones and which would be accidental. This is because an essential change is one that ends our existence, ends our numerical identity as the person we are. But then this must mean that the respect in which we change – the property that we lose in undergoing this change – is an essential property of us: a property without which we cannot be. So, we can find out what is essential to us, we can discover our deepest nature, by finding out which changes we could, and which we could not, survive.

And this, believe it or not, is precisely the way *Total Recall* works. Arnie undergoes a certain change – his memories are erased and new ones put in their places. The Verhoeven–Schwarzenegger claim, then, is that this is an essential change. The old person who was Arnie no longer exists; a new person has taken his place. This is why Arnie delivers his usual high body count. He is literally fighting for his life, his existence. Having the old memories – the memories of Hauser – put back in would literally end the existence of Quaid, the person he has become. So, Verhoeven–Schwarzenegger are defending what is often known as the *memory theory* of personal identity. If they are right, our memories are what are essential to us: what makes each one of us the same person from one day to the next, and what makes us different from anyone else, are our memories.

Are they right? First, let's look at some of the alternatives.

EMBODIED SOULS

Probably the most obvious alternative to the memory theory is what we can call the *soul theory*. According to this view, each one of us is essentially a soul. This soul has become embodied, housed in a physical vehicle – the body. But what is essential to each one of us is our soul. What makes you the same person now as you were yesterday, or last week, or last year, is that your soul is the same as it was yesterday, and last week, and last year. And what makes you the individual person you are, what guarantees your difference from anyone else, is the uniqueness of your soul.

Easy? But what exactly is a soul supposed to be? A simple *non-physical* object. That is, when people start invoking souls as an answer to the question of personal identity, they are, in effect, appealing to a form of what, as we saw in the last chapter, is known as *dualism*. And this is unfortunate since, as we also saw in the last chapter, dualism has a string of problems as long as your arm. The soul theory inherits all the problems of dualism.

Even if we could get around these problems, which we can't, there are further problems associated specifically with the use of the notion of a soul to explain issues of personal identity. The problem is that appeal to the soul makes it impossible for you to make any *justifiable judgments about a person's identity – even when that person is you.*

A judgment about identity is simply a judgment about who someone is. Suppose you see me, and engage in associated behaviour (muttering expletives to yourself, crossing the street to avoid me, etc.). Your actions are based on your judgment of who I am. But suppose the soul theory were true. How could you ever know who I am? Can you ever see, hear, feel, smell, taste or in any other way detect my soul? So, how do you know which soul is in there – wherever it is supposed to be?

Easy, you might think. You can judge who I am on the basis of my body, and using the principle that where there is the same body there is the same soul. You see my body, infer that this same body you met previously contains the same soul, so the same me, and hurry off across the street. But this only pushes the problem back. How could you ever have any reason to believe the principle that where there is the same body there is the same soul? How, that is, could you ever establish a correlation between body and soul?

To see the problem, think of your favourite beer. There you are with the six-pack of your choice. But how do you know the bottles contain the right beer? Well, of course, you get the bottles that have the appropriate label on them. But how do you establish a correlation between what's written on the outside of the bottle and what's contained on the inside? The point – and believe it or not there is a point – is that in order to establish a correlation between what's on the outside of the bottle and what's on the inside, you have to be able to open up the bottle and drink. You see the outside, open it up and enjoy the inside. And this illustrates a more general point. In order to establish a correlation between two things – no matter what they are – you must be able to establish independently the presence of both things. This is precisely what you can do in the case of beer. You see the outside. But then you open the bottle and independently establish through drinking and associated effects that the bottle contains your beer.

However, this is precisely what you can't do in the case of souls. You can't open up anyone's head – or anyone's anything else for that matter – and see the soul. Nor can you hear, smell, touch or taste their soul. Someone's soul is undetectable by anyone else. So, how can you establish a correlation between a soul and a body? You can't. Establishing a correlation between a soul and a body would be like establishing a correlation between the outside of a beer bottle and an invisible, intangible, tasteless – and therefore singularly uninteresting – beer that's supposedly inside.

Someone's soul, being a non-physical thing, is, even in principle, undetectable to anyone else. So you can't establish any correlation between souls and anything at all. Nothing. Nade. Zilch. Zip. But surely, you might think, this point only applies to other people. While we cannot detect the presence of someone else's soul, we all know of the presence of our own soul. So we can certainly establish a correlation between our own soul and our own body. And, since we have no reason for supposing that other people are any different from us, we can suppose that their souls are correlated with their bodies too.

This isn't going to work. For a start, to move from a claim about yourself to a claim about everyone else is a very weak sort of inference. It's like if you drank a bottle of your favourite beer, noted its pleasant effects, and inferred that every beer would have the same effects. Sorely disillusioned you would very quickly become. But there's an even more serious problem. Do we really know of the presence of our own soul? Remember the Hume–Nietzsche case against Descartes, described in Chapter 2. When we look in on ourselves, or introspect, all we come across are thoughts, feelings, emotions and stuff like that. We encounter only mental states, never any object which has those mental states. But the soul theory regards the soul as something separate from our mental states. Why? Because our mental states – our thoughts, feelings, desires, beliefs – are constantly changing. And it is supposedly the permanence and unchanging nature of the soul that underlies and unifies our shifting mental states, and thus makes us one, particular, person rather than a succession of different people. The soul, according to the soul theory, is not the same as mental states; it is the thing that *has* mental states, the object to which states of mind attach. But, when we introspect, we never come across any such object. All we come across are the mental states themselves, and not the thing that has them.

So, we have no means of establishing a correlation between body and soul – not in the case of other people and not even in our own case. Therefore, the soul theory is completely incapable of explaining our ability to make easy and accurate judgments about the identity of anyone – whether that person is someone else or whether that person is you.

JUSt a BODY?

The problems with the soul theory may make us opt for what is, in effect, the complete opposite view. This is known as the *body theory*. According to this view, what you are, essentially, is your body. You are the same person today as you were yesterday because you have the same body, and you are a different person from anyone else because you have a different body from anyone else.

Now, if you are thinking along the same lines as Heraclitus, you might say, 'Aha! But the body is never really the same. Body cells are constantly dying off and being replaced, or just dying.' I once had a friend who wanted to use this as a central plank in his petition for divorce, on the grounds that he was no longer the same person as the one who married his wife several years ago. A little philosophy is a dangerous thing. But, of course, this strategy is not going to work. Especially if the judge has read Aristotle. For we can just take Aristotle's line and regard this as a case of accidental change. The replacement, even the complete replacement, of body cells in a person's body no more ends the existence of that person than the complete replacement of water molecules in a river ends the existence of that river.

There is a more serious problem for the body theory, however. First of all, it seems very unlikely that the *whole* body goes into the identity of a person. To see this, consider this little-known fact: it is possible to cut heads off monkeys and apes, sew them back on to the bodies of other monkeys or apes, and keep the resulting combination alive. There is some scientist guy who goes around doing this. It's not clear why he does it, but he does. The resulting combination of head and body is, of course, paralysed from the neck down, but still alive and can be kept alive for a matter of weeks. This has been done. And if it is technically possible to do that with apes, it can also be done with human beings. Suppose this happened to you. Your head is cut off, sewn on to someone else's body, and the reverse is done with them – they get your body. Where would you be after this operation? Would you go where your head goes, or where your body goes? Now, I'm pretty sure, though I admit that this has never happened to me, that events would go something like this. You wake up, think 'What the fuck! What happened to my body? Why can't I move?' You would be staggered, stupefied, and not a little irked, to find that you have a new body, one that you cannot in any way move or influence. And this shows that you would be wherever your head is. The other person would be having similar thoughts and feelings, and that shows they would be where their head is.

If you're not convinced, suppose that one of the resulting combinations of head and body were to be destroyed. Suppose, for example, that the combination that involves your old body and the other person's head were destroyed. If you saw this, you might well rue the demise of your old body. But the fact that you could do this shows that you must still be around after its demise – otherwise you couldn't be rueing it. And if your body can be destroyed while you survive, then you cannot be the same thing as your body. That is, what is essential to you cannot be your whole body, because you could, in principle, survive its loss. Even with today's technology, this is possible. At most, it seems, the only thing you really need is your head: as long as it is attached to some body or other – doesn't matter which – you would survive.

But we can push this line of thought further. First of all, it's not really necessary that your head be attached to a body. What do you need a body for, anyway, if you're paralysed from the neck down? Not much use really, is it? The paralysed body is useful only to the extent that the blood and other chemicals that the brain needs to survive come through the body. With suitable technical advancement, it would presumably be possible, at least in principle, to supply these through other means. So, we might simply hook the head up to a tank of blood and stuff.

But then, do you really need your whole head? What if whoever it is who goes around cutting heads off and sewing them on to new bodies decided to remove bits of your head too? Your ears – you don't need them. After the surgery, you would wake up, think 'What the fuck etc. ... and where are my ears?' OK, we're getting rapidly into horror movie dimensions here – but what about your nose too? Same thing. You wake up, think 'What the fuck ... where are my ears ... and damn I don't remember being this ugly!'

In fact, if the head-switching guy was sufficiently accomplished, and found a way of maintaining blood supply to the brain and could counteract the effects of shock, haemorrhage, etc., then it seems he could take you down to your skull. Of course, you would no longer be able to see the effects, but you would probably be still in there wondering what the hell was going on. Technical limitations aside, you only need your skull because it is necessary to hold your brain in place, protect it and do various other container-type jobs. If, for example, it were possible to find an alternative means of performing the same thing – a plastic skull, for example – then the head-switcher could dispense with your skull too. Or, instead of a plastic skull, what if he just floated your brain in a vat of suitable nutrients – ones that would keep the brain alive and functioning? Remember this from Chapter 2? So, it can't be your body that is essential to who you are. You could, in principle, lose that and still be the same person – though presumably a seriously pissed off version of your former self. And so we arrive at the next account of personal identity: the brain theory.

are you your brain?

According to the brain theory, what is essential to you is your brain. Of course, we're not just brains: we have bodies too. And what this means is that all your other bodily features are basically accidental ones – accidental in Aristotle's sense. That is, you could survive the loss of all your other features, but not the loss of your brain. In fact, we just imagined a situation where you could lose all your other features and survive because your brain survives.

According to the brain theory, then, you're the same person today as you were yesterday or ten years ago because you have the same brain – and the loss of a depressingly large number of brain cells in the intervening years can be written off as an accidental, rather than essential, change. And what makes you the person you are and not anyone else is the fact that no one else has your brain.

Are we really our brains? Is that what's essential to us? Well, what is the brain? A complex, organic, electrical and chemical system. Now, suppose you're depressed? This may well be because of some chemical imbalance – say a deficiency in serotonin. So, you take pills that increase the amount of serotonin in your brain. There's no problem in introducing chemical substances that have not been produced by you. This does not make you a different person – not in the *numerical* sense of different. It just makes you a happier person, that's all.

But now let's consider a more radical possibility: a change in the physical composition of your brain. What does a neuron do? Basically, it receives electro-chemical messages from some other neurons, and sends them on to others. That's all. So, in principle at least, it should be possible to construct something else that does the same job. Now, suppose that your brain, like that of the author, is deteriorating. Neurons are dying, and not being replaced. Suppose, through an improvement in magnetic resonance imaging techniques, or whatever, we are able to identify the dying neurons as they die. Then we might be able to replace them, on a one-by-one basis, with artificial neurons. To make this most plausible, we can focus on a treatment that is already being developed. Certain types of degenerative brain conditions, like Alzheimer's and Parkinson's disease can, it seems likely, be treated by the implantation of foetal stem cells. These cells are used because they are, to use the industry term, extremely *plastic*. That is, they are very flexible – the way they develop and what they do can vary greatly. So, when implanted in a degenerating brain, they can, theoretically, take on the role of the dead neurons, and the neural connections that would otherwise be lost can be preserved.

Suppose this happened to you. It is implausible to suppose that this is tantamount to death – that the person who existed before the implantation is no longer, and that a new person has taken their place. On the contrary, the implantation, it seems most plausible to assume, is precisely what keeps you in existence. And this would be true even if every single cell in your brain were replaced by foetal stem cells. In some ways, this is similar to the case of other body cells, which replace themselves every seven years or so. But there is a difference, the new body cells are ones produced by you, but these new brain cells are introduced from the outside, from somebody else.

We could imagine a situation where this sort of replacement procedure is carried out progressively, so that over a certain period of time, all of your original brain cells are replaced by foetal trans-plant cells. As long as the implanted foetal cells preserved the original functioning of your original brain cells – so that your thoughts, memories, feelings, sense of self were preserved – it seems you would survive, just as you would survive a case of par-tial foetal cell implantation. But in what sense do you have the same brain as the one you originally had? Unlike the case of ordi-nary body cell replacement, these new cells are not ones created by you, they have been introduced from the outside, from some-one else. So it's not clear that you still have your original brain. On the other hand, it's not really clear that you don't.

Let's consider a slightly more radical alternative. The new cells introduced into your brain are organic, but they are not foetal stem cells, but ones, let's suppose, specifically engineered for the purpose. They are ones created in the laboratory, in the test tube, and then introduced into your degenerating brain. This may, of course, never be technically possible, but it's the principle we are after. And the principle remains the same. As long as the intro-duced cells preserve the same function as the original ones, you will survive the implantation. I mean, look at it from your per-spective, as the one undergoing the procedure. Everything will seem the same after the procedure as before it. All your thoughts, feelings, memories will be the same (or seem the same) because your new brain is doing exactly the same things as the old brain and in the same environment. So, from your perspective, nothing will have changed. You may acquire new beliefs in the process – like 'Phew, I've survived the operation.' But that's about it.

The conclusion we seem to be driven towards is something

like this. From the point of view of our identity, it's not so much what the brain *is* that's important but what it *does*. If we could find some replacement – based on foetal stem cells, artificially constructed organic or inorganic chips, etc. – that did exactly the same things as our original brain, then, it seems, we would survive. So our identity is carried by what the brain *does* rather than what it *is*. What does the brain do? It houses our mental states – our thoughts, feelings, beliefs, desires, emotions, hopes, fears, expectations and, crucially, our memories. And so we arrive, more or less, at the Verhoeven–Schwarzenegger *memory theory*.

ᏋᎻᎬ ᎷᎬᎷᎾᎡᎽ ᎢᎻᎬᎾᎡᎽ

Actually, the memory theory is not a good name. There are loads and loads of mental states involved. Arnie, for example, when he is Quaid, has, in addition to new memories, various new beliefs, such as believing that he has been married for eight years and that Sharon Stone is his wife. He has new emotions – an attachment to Ms Stone, for example. But memories are central in that the reason he has these new other mental states is, at least arguably, because of the memories that have been put in him. So we can call it the memory theory, although it's often called the *psychological continuity theory*.

According to the memory theory, each one of us is, essentially, a bundle of memories and related psychological states – beliefs, thoughts, emotions, hopes, fears. That's what makes us the persons we are. Quaid is, therefore, a completely different person from Hauser, it's just that both of them, at different times, occupied the same body. Verhoeven–Schwarzenegger emphasise this very cleverly in the scene where Quaid is strapped into the machine that will erase his memories and restore Hauser's in their place. As Arnie flexes his massive biceps, struggling to break the wrist straps that hold him in place, he is literally struggling for his very existence. The memory replacement is tantamount to death – it will end his existence as the person he is.

Hauser, i.e. evil Arnie, emphasises this point when, in his recorded message to Quaid, he says, 'I wish I could wish you a long life and happiness. But that can't be, because I need my body back.' Therefore, when Quaid does break free, and graphically stabs various technicians through the head with steel rods that have conveniently broken off from the chair to which he was strapped, this is not gratuitous violence. Verhoeven–Schwarzenegger are making a sophisticated philosophical point about the relationship between memories and personal identity. In fact, I think, in the history of philosophy, no more convincing case has ever been made for the memory theory. Good philosophers like John Locke can carp on about the memories of princes being put into the bodies of cobblers, and stuff like that. But not until you see Arnie defending – with extreme prejudice – his new identity at the expense of his old do you appreciate the full force of the memory theory.

THE SIXTH DAY AND THE PROBLEM OF FISSION

When I first saw *Total Recall* in the cinema, I remember saying to my girlfriend of the time, 'What a pity they didn't address the problem of fission!' Unaccountably, she left me soon afterwards.

But the problem of fission, or the problem of duplication as it's sometimes called, is a big problem for the memory theory. And that's a big problem all round – because the memory theory is the only remotely plausible account of personal identity we've got. I was slightly disappointed in Arnie that he seemed not to have even considered this objection to his otherwise cogent case. But I should not have doubted the big man. Ten years later, in the Roger Spottiswoode film *The Sixth Day* (2000), he develops an intriguing account of the major problem with the memory theory. And here, I think it is fair to say, we notice an important shift in his philosophical position. He moves away from the Aristotelian idea of a stable and persisting self towards the Heraclitean view that there is no such thing as the self or person.

It is some time in the near future ('Sooner than you think!') and Adam Gibson is a disgustingly happy family man, with a beautiful and adoring wife and a cloyingly sweet little daughter. Why did Arnie have to start portraying these family men all the time? What was wrong with being a terminator, or a commando, or a mercenary kicking the butt of an extraterrestrial on a hunting trip? Anyway, for Adam Gibson, all is rosy in the garden. Until, that is, he returns to his house one day to find that he is already there. Or rather, somebody that looks exactly like him is already there. The agents who turn up to terminate the rather shocked Arnie, just as he is about to go into the house and confront his doppelgänger, explain: 'There's been a Sixth Day violation. A human was cloned. That human was you.' Then they try to kill him. But he, of course, escapes and kills a few of the agents. Then he goes off to find out what's what while his clone stays behind, smokes his cigars, and shags his wife in the back of his car. Ouch!

The cloning technology in *The Sixth Day*, spearheaded by Robert Duvall, is somewhat under-explained, but seems to involve two essential stages. First a DNA sample is taken and implanted into a purpose-grown 'blank' – a vaguely human body minus any 'specific' DNA – whatever that means. Secondly, a *cerebral syncording* is taken, by way of a device that looks like it is supposed to test eyes. I would really like to know how this works, but the basic idea seems to be that it reads off a total picture of the brain in all its states, and thus stores the thoughts, memories, etc. contained in that brain. So, your mental states are stored on disk.

Anyway, the cloning of Arnie was a mistake. He was supposed to have been killed in an attack by some anti-cloning religious fundamentalists on the chief cloning baddie, Tony Goldwyn. Arnie was supposed to pilot the guy on a skiing trip. But Arnie never went, he sent Michael Rapaport instead, while Arnie went off to look into having his dead pet dog cloned so his daughter wouldn't be upset on his birthday. So, to cover up the attack – since the chief cloning baddie was cloned – Arnie was cloned too. So, two Arnies instead of one. Hence the problem. Human cloning is illegal, and the cloning baddies have to cover up what they've done.

Anyway, as you have probably guessed – it all turns out all right in the end. More or less anyway, and plus or minus a twist or two that I won't spoil for you now. The original Arnie stays behind to shag his wife and love his kids, and the cloned Arnie goes off to sea, a division of responsibilities which, in my view, cloned Arnie is surprisingly willing to accept. (And, if he had bothered to watch *Total Recall*'s defence of the memory theory, he would know why.)

For our purposes, the storyline does not quite work. Suppose we ask the question, 'Who is the real Adam Gibson?' Chances are we'll come up with the answer: 'The one who was around first.' The fact that one Adam Gibson was around before the other strongly suggests that the first one is kosher, and the second one a mere copy. So, let's amend the story slightly. Let's suppose, as the cloning baddies assumed, that the body of the original Adam Gibson is destroyed, and his memories are implanted into a custom-made clone. Does Adam Gibson survive? Or, rather, if the memory theory is true, does this mean that Adam Gibson survives? What does the memory theory imply?

Well, pretty clearly, it implies that the clone with Adam Gibson's memories is, in fact, Adam Gibson. Because what we are, according to the memory theory, is a collection of memories and other mental states – beliefs, desires, thoughts, emotions and the like. And if these are preserved, we are preserved. Simple as that. Actually, it's not *quite* as simple as that. We are all familiar with the idea of false or apparent memories – things that *seem* like memories, but are not the real thing. If I seem to remember winning the battle of Austerlitz, turning over the running of the battle at Waterloo to that idiot Maréchal Ney, and being banished to St Helena, then, pretty clearly, I'm deluded. These memories are clearly not kosher. And no sensible version of the memory theory would want to entail that I am, in fact, Napoleon. To avoid this, we have to distinguish real from merely apparent memories, pseudo-memories if you like. The memory theory applies only to real memories. That is, what goes into determining your identity are real memories, and not pseudo-memories.

In the case of the Adam Gibson clone, are the memories real ones or merely pseudo-memories? Well, what is it that makes a memory real as opposed to merely apparent? Basically, the difference seems to be that real memories are ones that are actually caused by the things that they are memories of. In the case of pseudo-memories, there is no such causal link. Napoleon could remember winning the battle of Austerlitz because his memory was caused by his winning the battle. I can't remember winning the battle of Austerlitz, no matter how much it seems to me as if I can, because I was never actually there. Therefore, all I can have is apparent memories of winning the battle.

If the difference between real memories and apparent or pseudo-memories comes down to this sort of causal connection, then the memories of the cloned Adam Gibson are just as real as those of the original Adam Gibson. When cloned Adam Gibson remembers that he has stashed some – now illegal – cigars in his car, there is a clear causal connection between this memory and the cigars actually being put in the car. This causal connection is slightly non-standard because it incorporates two brains, rather than the one brain involved in more standard cases. Nonetheless, the memory in cloned Adam Gibson's brain is caused by the memory in original Adam Gibson's brain, and the memory in original Adam Gibson's brain is caused by his stashing the cigars in the car. So, we have a clear causal connection between cloned

Adam Gibson's memory and the cigars being stashed in the car. And so cloned Adam Gibson's memory qualifies as a real memory rather than a pseudo-memory.

So, according to the memory theory, cloned Adam Gibson is one and the same person as the original Adam Gibson. In our imagined case where the anti-cloning fundamentalists did destroy the original Adam Gibson, and not his unlucky partner Michael Rapaport, then the Adam Gibson would survive as his clone. Original Adam Gibson, according to the memory theory, *is* his clone. Original Adam Gibson and cloned Adam Gibson are one and the same person.

But, now, suppose that someone fucks up on the cloning production line, and not one but two clones are made. Adam Gibson's memories are implanted in both of them. Which one is the real Adam Gibson? Now, we have a problem: it's called the *problem of fission*, or *duplication problem*. The problem is that each clone, according to the memory theory, seems to have *equal* claim to be Adam Gibson. Both have his memories, and these memories seem to be real ones – ones that are causally connected to the events of which they are memories. So, no one clone has any more or any less right to be regarded as Adam Gibson than the other. But, and here's the rub, *both* of them can't be Adam Gibson. Why not? Because Adam Gibson is one person, and the two clones are not one person, and one person cannot be two persons.

Why are the two clones different people? Well, they have different properties. They can go off, do completely different things. One, for example, can stay behind, shag Adam's wife, buy his daughter presents, and stuff like that, while the other can go off to sea to be killed in a freak accident. One of them can die, while the other survives – so they have to be two different people.

Why can't one person be two? Well, just as part of the general principle that one thing cannot be two things. One person cannot be two people any more than one bottle of beer can be two bottles of beer. Adam Gibson, before the cloning took place, was one person. Therefore, he cannot be identical with – the same thing as – two people.

So, here's the problem. Adam Gibson cannot be both clones. One person cannot be two. But no clone has any greater right to be regarded as Adam Gibson than the other. There's no basis, for example, for saying that Adam Gibson is clone 1 rather than clone 2, or vice versa. He can't be both, but neither can he really be one rather than the other. So what are we to say? Does Adam Gibson not survive the procedure after all?

But this is kind of silly too. Put yourself in his position. You wake up one morning – say the morning of 23 July 2004, and everything seems normal. You know you were cloned last night, and your original body destroyed, but good memory theorist that you are, this does not bother you one bit. Memories have been preserved, and this, you believe, makes you the same person as the one who existed before the cloning. You then go on and live a happy and fulfilled life for, say, the next 20 years. But then, on the morning of 23 July 2024, you discover that 20 years ago you were, in fact, not the only clone made. Due to some glitch in the cloning procedure, two clones were made. But now, you realise, neither you nor your clone double have any greater right to be the original person – Adam. But Adam was one person and he cannot be the same as both of you. So, what do you conclude? Did your existence end on the cloning table all those years ago? Your existence ended, it's just that you didn't realise it? To answer yes seems silly.

This is the problem. According to the memory theory, preservation of memories and psychological continuity in general entails preservation of the person. You survive, so long as your memories and other psychological states do. So, if your memories etc. are successfully implanted into a clone, say, then you survive. The procedure has, from the point of view of your survival, been a success. But, if your memories and other psychological states are implanted into two clones, how can you reasonably be thought not to survive? How can a *double success* add up to a *failure*?

The short answer is: *it can't*. But this is only the tip of the gigantic iceberg of a problem that's beginning to emerge here. If only one clone is created, the memory theory seems committed to saying that the clone is the same person as the original. But if two clones are created, the memory theory cannot say that the two clones are the same as the original person. *Must* and *can't* again – the hallmark of a nasty philosophical problem. But – and this is the crux of the matter – how can the status of one clone as the same or different from the original Adam possibly depend on whether or not *another* clone was created? Surely, it should depend only on the nature of the individual clone – on whether the memories of the original Adam are preserved. How can it depend on whether someone on the cloning production line accidentally pushed the 'clone' button twice instead of once?

The answer, again, is: *it can't*. We're confused on something. And our confusion reveals something deeply disturbing about us. There is no us.

ᏕᎻᎬ ᏒᎥᏌᎬᏒ ᎧᏞ ᏕᎬᏞᏌᎬᏕ

Each one of us, it seems, is a person. And we have been trying to work out what it is to be a person. To work this out, we posed the questions: what makes us the *same* person from one day to the next, and what makes us a *different* person from anyone else? And our attempts to answer this have led us into total paradox. The only remotely plausible account of persons that we have – the memory theory – led us to the paradoxical conclusion that Adam Gibson both *must* be his clone and *can't* be his clone.

The root of the problem, I think, lies with the notions of *sameness* and *difference*. For these are bound up with the concept of identity – and it is this that is leading us astray. To ask, for example, what makes me the same person from one day to the next presupposes that I am the same person from one day to the next. It presupposes that I have an identity that persists through time. And to ask what makes me a different person from anyone else presupposes that I am the sort of thing whose identity can be separated off from that of anyone else. So, the way we have been asking the question presupposes that some sort of absolute notion of sameness, and so some absolute notion of identity, can be applied to persons. The problem is that this sort of way of thinking about persons leads us into paradox.

What if we are not this sort of thing at all. What if, that is, the concept of identity is just inappropriate for thinking about you and me and other persons. What if, that is, the concept of *identity* and the concept of a *person* just don't *fit* each other. I think that this is what Arnie, in his later work, is trying to get us to realise. The concept of identity just does not apply to persons. If we want to understand what we are, then we have to stop using the concept of identity. We are simply not the sorts of things that can have an identity through time. I am not identical with – I am not the same person as – the me of last year, or last week, or even yesterday. There is no me that persists through time, or which is different, in any absolute sense, from you.

Instead of thinking of persons in terms of identity – what makes you the *same* person from day to day, what makes you *different* from anyone else – think of them in terms of the notion of *survival*. There is nothing, nothing at all, that makes you the same person from day to day. And there is nothing, nothing in any absolute sense, that makes you different from everyone else. Rather, the you of today is a *survivor*, a very *close survivor*, of the you of yesterday. It is a survivor, though a slightly more distant survivor, of the you of last week, and a much more distant survivor of the you of last year. In a single body is not one self or person, but a succession of selves, a river of selves, each one a survivor of the one that went before. To the extent we can talk of *the* self, we are talking of something that has the character of a river, of a process, not a thing.

If we accept this, then we have a neat explanation of the duplication objection. Neither clone 1 nor clone 2 is *identical* with Adam Gibson. But they are both very close *survivors* of Adam Gibson. This should not make Arnie sad. None of us is ever identical with ourselves – we are all just survivors, very close survivors of the person we were a moment ago. There is no you – there is just a succession of *yous*, all of which are very, very close descendants of the you that preceded them.

What does this idea of *survival* mean here? We can explain it in terms of the idea of psychological continuity. Consider the memories, beliefs, thoughts, desires, emotions that you have today. Say now. Then, a minute ago, the memories, beliefs, thoughts, desires, emotions and other mental states that you had will be almost exactly the same as the ones you have now. There will be slight divergences, but the overlap is almost total. Because of this overwhelming psychological continuity between the you of now and the you of a minute ago, we can say that the you of now is a very close survivor of the you of a minute ago. Now, take the you of a particular moment last week. Still, the psychological overlap or continuity between the you of now and the you of last week will be large, but not as great as it is between the you of now and the you of a minute ago. Although you will still share large numbers of memories, beliefs and other psychological states, in the space of a week you will have acquired more new beliefs, more new desires, more new memories than you could have acquired in the space of a minute. So, although you are a close survivor of the you of that moment last week, you are not as close to this previous you as you are to the you of a minute ago. The further you go back in time, the greater grows the psychological discontinuity, and the more distant a relative to the present you does the previous you become.

And that, I think, is all there is to us. We are not – literally not – the same person from one time to the next, nor are we absolutely different from anyone else. We are all a constant flow, a succession, of persons, each one is closely bound to the one that immediately preceded it, and less and less closely bound to the ones that preceded that, and so on. You go back long enough, you may have virtually nothing in common with the person you find there. In the end, Heraclitus's analogy of the river wasn't far off the mark after all, but this is for very different reasons than those advanced by Heraclitus. It's not just that we are constantly changing. Everything is constantly changing, and we have no problems applying the concept of identity to most things. Persons, however, are special things. The attempt to apply the concept of identity to persons leads to paradox. The most natural explanation of this is that the concept is unsuited to persons, that it cannot be legitimately applied to them, and so that a person is not the sort of thing that has an identity in space or through time.

Inside and Outside Again

In the issue of personal identity we again find our clash of the view from the inside and the view from the outside. From the inside I seem, to myself, to be a particular and unique person, a centre of consciousness that is distinct and different from any other centre of consciousness, and that persists through time. I am who I am, I am no one else, and I have been who I am for getting on for forty years now. Sure, I may have changed over that time, but I – the essential I – have persisted through those changes. But when I look at my identity from the outside, I can find no such thing. I can find, that is, nothing that corresponds to the view that I have from the inside. From the outside, there is, and can be, no me. At best, there is simply a succession of *me*s, a stream or river of *I*s which succeed each other with a seamless but astonishing rapidity. From the inside I am stable and unique; there is something that underlies and persists through whatever changes I undergo. From the outside there is nothing that meets this description. From the inside I have to be a certain way, from the outside I can't be that way – indeed, there is no I there to be or not be that way. And this is the problem of personal identity.

5) MINORITY REPORT
the problem of free will

tom cruise's philosophical awakening

Minority Report (2002) is Steven Spielberg's interpretation of another story by the great Philip K. Dick. In many ways, it's a strange film. Unlike most films that raise complex philosophical issues, there's not a lot of graphic violence in it. It also has Tom Cruise in it, not a man you normally associate with complex philosophical issues. I mean, scientology? Give me a break. If the central premise of this book is correct, then the philosophical merit of a position is directly proportional to how well that position can be translated into a *sci-phi* movie. And did anyone see *Battlefield Earth*? A film that made even the prodigiously talented John Travolta look like he belonged in the local amateur rep.

Nevertheless, despite his somewhat shaky track record, we now see signs of a philosophical awakening in Tom. Did Penelope Cruz awaken him from his dogmatic slumbers, perhaps? His recent *Vanilla Skies* (2002), for example, provided an interesting examination of the sort of Cartesian epistemological themes we looked at in Chapter 2. And in *Minority Report* Tom has managed to star in a film that has genuine philosophical merit and originality. Complex philosophical ideas there are aplenty here. Most importantly, it provides a good investigation of the problem of freedom, or, as philosophers are prone to putting it – the problem of *freedom of the will*.

Once again, this is a problem that develops out of the clash between the two views we have of ourselves – the inner and the outer. From the inside, what could be more obvious than the fact of our free will? What could be more obvious than the fact that we are capable of choosing and acting freely? From the inside, when a situation arises, we often find ourselves with a choice about how to respond. We make our choice, and we act. And, usually, we do so freely. It's not as if anybody has a gun to our head, at least not typically. From the inside, then, what could be more obvious than the fact that we have free will? We *must* have free will, we can scarcely imagine not having free will. At least, so it seems to us.

But, as we shall see, from the outside, we have huge problems even making sense of this thing – free will – that we are supposed to have. From the outside, we don't seem to be able to find anything there that corresponds to the thing that, from the inside, we take ourselves to plainly have. From the outside, we *can't* have free will – there is nothing there for us to have.

So, we must, we feel, be free, but we can't possibly see how we could be. Inside and outside. Must and can't. Once again, a nasty philosophical problem.

MINORITY REPORT

The year is 2054. In the years running up to this, murders had apparently spiralled out of control. However, a way of stopping them has somewhat implausibly arisen, apparently the result of past misadventures with yet to be invented hallucinogens by various pregnant women, resulting in neural-genetic abnormalities in their children who are, as a consequence, able to foretell the future – or, at least, those parts of the future that involve murders. No, don't laugh, it could happen. Most of these precognisant children – *precogs*, as they are known in the film – apparently die from an inability to distinguish the present from the murderous future, and the resulting stress that this inability inevitably occasions. However, three survive. They are then promptly (1) named after three murder writers – Arthur, after Arthur Conan Doyle; Dashiel, after Dashiel Hammett; and, the most talented of the three, Agatha, after Agatha Christie; (2) heavily drugged; (3) made to float around in a swimming pool; and (4) put to work predicting murders before they happen.

Built up around them is a new police department – the Pre-Crime Unit – led by John Anderton (Tom Cruise reprising his usual role of Cocky Bastard who later comes to understand the dignity and worth of human beings), and overseen by Lamar Burgess (Max von Sydow who, since it's Max von Sydow, is obviously going to turn out to be an Evil Bastard).

Anyway, to cut a long story short, the precogs predict a murder. It's going to take place in 72 hours, and, unfortunately for Tom, he's the perp. He's going to kill a guy called Leo Crow – someone he's never heard of before. You see, Tom's son was abducted and presumably killed some six years previously. Tom was, at the time, holding his breath at the bottom of a swimming pool, and when he came up for air, his boy had gone. And, understandably, he never really got over it. Crow is pretty obviously supposed to be the killer. Or so we think. But, clever plot twist or what, he's not really the killer. He's been paid, by some unknown interloper, to let Tom kill him, with the idea that his family will get the money. But Tom, striking a blow for human freedom and dignity everywhere, *doesn't* in fact kill him. You see, he is human and so has a *choice*. This doesn't help him very much, since he's eventually apprehended by his own Pre-Crime unit, and put in suspended animation indefinitely.

Of course, it all turns out OK in the end (this is, after all, a Spielberg movie). He gets his wife back and even manages to impregnate her. Max von Sydow is unmasked as the principal baddie and, honourably, kills himself. And the precogs, and everybody they've convicted, all live happily ever after. What's going on here?

the captain of my fate?

Actually, what's going on is an interesting and subtle exploration of the age-old philosophical problem of free will. Most of the chapter I'm going to spend trying to convince you that there *is* a problem. Once you're convinced, you'll see what a big and bad-assed problem it is.

You are wired up to an electroencephalogram which records brain activity at a number of points on your head. A researcher asks you to flex your index finger a few times, but to do this suddenly at moments that are entirely of your own choosing. At the time you choose to move your finger, you are asked to note the positioning of a clock hand. If this happened to you, then you were probably the subject of a classic series of experiments conducted by Benjamin Libet. Or, if you are old enough, you may have appeared in essentially the same experiments performed earlier by H. H. Kornhuber. Whichever experiment you were in, the results would have probably come as something of a surprise to you. Whereas your conscious decision to move your finger occurred only a fraction of a second before you moved it, the recorded electrical activity in your brain, measured by the electro-encephalogram, gradually built up a second to a second and a half before you flexed your finger. The decision to move your finger, that is, appears to occur *after* the brain activity that causes your finger to move.

The Libet/Kornhuber experiment is one of those things that makes you go *hmmm* ... For at least on one interpretation of its results, it seems to show that your sense that your finger moved because of a conscious and free act of your will is an illusion. The movement of your finger was actually caused by the activity in your brain, activity which occurred before your act of will, and of which you were completely unaware. Now I'm not saying this is the only interpretation of the results of this experiment. There are others (more or less desperate in my opinion). But, it does make you think. And that is good enough to start.

We all have this idea that we are free. By this, I am not talking about political freedom. Political freedom has to do with how much the government or society lets us do what we want, and how much they should let us do what we want, and stuff like that. The freedom we are going to talk about is much more fundamental than that. Suppose government or society said: 'Go ahead, knock yourself out, do anything you want …. and we really mean anything!' Then there would still be an issue of freedom in the sense we are going to talk about. Because this issue is about whether we can ever really freely choose anything at all, even if there is nobody there to prevent us. The sense of freedom we are after is much deeper than political freedom. What we're after is what's sometimes called *metaphysical* freedom.

ᏟᎻᎬ PᎡOBᏞᎬᎷ OF FᎡᎬᎬDOᎷ

In the Libet experiments, let's contrast the view from the inside with the view from the outside. From the inside, the decision to move your finger is a decision you freely make. This decision results in an act of will – or, as we put it in philosophy, a *volition* – and as a result of this act of will, you move your finger. Since your decision is one you freely make, and since the act of will is something you freely form, so too is the action of moving your finger one that is freely performed. So, the view from the inside is probably a variation on this sort of theme:

> **decision/choice** *that is freely made results in*
> **volition** *that is freely formed and this results in*
> **action** *that is freely performed.*

Actions are free because they are the result of decisions/choices and volitions or acts of will that are freely chosen and formed by you. Your actions are free because they are the result of your free decisions and volitions.

The story from the outside, however, contradicts this story

from the inside in two different ways. First, the story from the outside challenges the idea that our actions are the result of our decisions and volitions. This is what is so disturbing about the Libet experiments. The activity in your brain that caused your finger to move seems to occur, at least in part, before either your decision or your volition to move your finger. Both the decision to move your finger and the act of will that your finger move seem to occur after the activity in your brain that, in fact, causes your finger to move. So, the Libet experiments suggest that it is, in fact, neither a decision nor an act of will on your part that causes your finger to move. It is brain activity that is relevant to the production of your action, and not, as we commonly suppose, the conscious decisions and volitions that you make and form.

But there is another, even deeper, way in which the story from the outside contradicts the story from the inside. The story from the outside tells us that each one of us is simply another thing in the world, subject to the same causal forces and processes that produce and control everything else. And a consequence of this is that *even if* actions were produced by things such as decisions and acts of will, this would not be enough to make those actions free – for the simple reason that we do not have any control over our decisions and acts of will.

For example, you're now reading this book. This is an action on your part. Is this action something that you freely chose to do? Well, it's unlikely that someone has a gun to your head, and hopefully sales won't be so bad that I'll have to contemplate that type of marketing approach. But suppose the marketing people at Ebury decided to boost rather sluggish sales by hypnotising you:

hypnotically inducing into you an uncontrollable desire to read the book. And suppose the desire thus induced was so strong that there was no way you could fight it. You had to satisfy the desire, and the only way to do it was by reading the book. In this sort of scenario, you don't really have any control over your action. Why not? Because your decision to read the book, and thus your action, is the inevitable result of an overwhelmingly powerful desire you have, and this is not a desire over which you have any control. Some sod hypnotically induced it in you. So, if you don't have any control over the desire, then neither do you have any control over the inevitable results of the desire, in this case the decision to read the book and the action of reading the book. More generally, if you don't have control over the causes of your actions, and if your actions are the inevitable result of these causes, then you don't have any control over the actions either.

Are there any reasons for thinking that we don't have control over the causes of our actions? Yes, and they're provided by a neat little argument in support of what's known as *determinism*. And determinism, in effect, is what *Minority Report* is all about.

Determinism

Determinism can be defined as the combination of two claims. The first is a claim about causation, the second a consequence this is thought to have for human freedom:

1.   Everything that exists or occurs, including human actions, choices and decisions, has a cause.
2.   Therefore, human actions, choices and decisions are not free.

The first thing we have to do is understand why determinists think claim (2) follows from claim (1).

The basic idea connecting (1) and (2) is this: *causes make their effects inevitable*. It's necessary here to distinguish between what we can call *partial* causes and *total* causes. A spark, for example, might be the cause of an explosion, but it is only a partial cause. In order for the explosion to happen, the spark must also occur in the presence of combustible gases, in the presence of enough oxygen, and on it goes. Actually, I have no idea of the total list of conditions that have to be met in order for the explosion to occur, but you can bet that there is such a list. This list: spark, combustible gases, oxygen, plus whatever else is required, we can call the total cause of the explosion. And the idea is that if the total cause of the explosion occurs, then the explosion *must* also occur. Given the existence of the total cause, the explosion is made inevitable.

So, the idea underlying determinism is that *total* causes make their effects inevitable. And similarly, when determinists say that everything that exists or occurs has a cause, what they mean is that it has a total cause. In order not to have to write 'total cause' all the time, from now on when I talk about causes, you can understand me as referring to total causes. If I have to talk about partial causes for any reason, then I shall explicitly say 'partial cause'.

So, if determinism is right, everything which exists or occurs has a (total) cause; and this includes human actions, choices and decisions, since these are things which occur. So, take an action of yours, say the action of reading this book. Do you have control over this action? Well, if determinism is right, your action will have a (total) cause, and this makes the action inevitable. That is, given the cause occurs, your action must occur. What sort of thing might this cause be? Well, typically, it might, for example, be a decision: say the decision to read the book. Actually, it's probably a mistake to think of the action as being caused by just one thing. As in the case of the explosion, there are probably many factors which go into the (total) cause, and, indeed, the case of action might be much more complex than that of the explosion. But, just for simplicity's sake, let's suppose that the cause of your action is simply your decision. Nothing of any importance turns on this simplification.

So, your action is, let's suppose, (totally) caused by your decision. This means that if your decision occurs, your action is inevitable. And this means that unless you have control over your decision, you don't have any control over the action either. If the decision makes the action inevitable, and if you have no control over the decision, then you can't have any control over the action either. How could you? This is why if the decision to read the book has been hypnotically induced in you then your action of reading the book is not a free action. The action is not free because the decision is not free, and the decision makes the action inevitable.

Do you have any control over the decision? Well, remember that according to determinism, everything that exists or occurs has a cause. So your decision also has a cause (a total cause, remember), and this makes the decision inevitable. So, if you don't have any control over this cause, then you won't have any control over the decision either. If, for example, the cause of your decision to read the book was a hypnotically induced desire to read it and you had no control over this desire, then you wouldn't have any control over the decision either, since this, we are supposing, is the inevitable result of the desire. So the action is not free because the decision is not free, and the decision is not free because the desire is not free.

But remember, according to determinism, everything that exists or occurs has a cause. So the desire would, in turn, have a cause too. And in order to have any control over the desire, we must have control over the cause of the desire. In the case of the hypnotically induced desire, we have no such control, and this is why we regard the desire – and all that ensues from it – as not free. I could go on, literally *ad infinitum*, but you probably get the picture by now. The picture we can represent as a line or lineage of causes:

$$..... E_1 - E_2 - E_3 - E_4 - E_5 .....$$

This is just a small segment of the line. The line is infinitely long. Or, if time has a beginning and end, then the line stretches back to the beginning of time and on to the end of time.

The question is this. Do you have control over event 5? Well, only if you have control over event 4, since event 4 is the (total) cause of event 5 and so makes it inevitable. Do you have control over event 4? Well, only if you have control over event 3, since event 3 is the total cause over event 4, and so makes it inevitable. And so on. Event 5 might be the action of reading this book. Event 4 would then be the decision to read it. Event 3 would be the desire to read it. Event 2 would be the cause of the desire. And event 1 would be the cause of the cause of the desire.

The thing is this. For any one of our actions, we can trace the line of causes of that action back indefinitely far, in principle to the beginning of the universe, or for ever if the universe had no beginning. Now, at some stage in this sequence of causes, we are surely going to reach a cause over which we have no control. Once we reach our early childhood, or infancy, then it seems very likely that the causes which affect us are ones over which we have no control. And even if you want to claim that you have control over the causes that occurred in your early childhood, or even infancy, pretty clearly you can't have control over causes that occurred before you were born. Whatever the point at which we reach them is, we must eventually reach causes over which we have no control since we must eventually reach causes that occurred before we even existed, and which played a role in beginning and shaping our existence. And we clearly cannot have any control over these sorts of causes.

However, if at any point we reach a cause over which we have no control, then neither can we have any control over anything which follows that cause in the sequence. This is because, as we have seen, causes make their effects inevitable. So, if, for example, we have no control over E_1, then we have no control over E_2 either, since E_2 is the inevitable result of E_1. But, therefore, neither do we have any control over E_3 since this is the inevitable result of E_2, and so on. If we have no control over an event, then we have no control over anything which that event makes inevitable.

Now, if, as the determinist says, everything that exists or occurs has a cause, then every action we take, and every choice and decision we make, will have causes. And these causes will have causes. And these causes of causes will have causes. Eventually, we must arrive at causes over which we have no control. Therefore, we have no control over the choices, decisions and actions that, eventually, result from them. And this, in essence, completes the argument for determinism.

You might think that the appearance of a problem here stems merely from the fact that I'm being hopelessly over-simplistic. And, admittedly, it wouldn't be the first time. In particular, you might feel like pointing out that the idea of there being one line or causal lineage stretching forwards and backwards in time is too crude. And, of course, it is. There won't be one line, there will be a myriad of intersecting lines, criss-crossing each other with un-believable complexity. One causal sequence will inevitably inter-sect, traverse and overlap with many others, ones which in turn intersect others etc. So, each one of our lives would involve us fol-lowing an indefinite number of potential lines. And each one of our actions would involve us potentially following an indefinite number of causal sequences. So, why couldn't the element of free choice come in here? When you decide to do something, for example, why couldn't the freedom of your choice consist in your following one causal sequence rather than another?

Unfortunately for human freedom and dignity, this isn't going to work. Suppose, at any point in time, there is a labyrinth of intersecting causal sequences, various lineages of one event causing another, which in turns causes another, with all these lines traversing each other with a degree of complexity that it is, per-haps, impossible for us to grasp. The suggestion is that free choice comes in with the decision to follow one causal lineage rather than another. Suppose you opt for lineage *n*, whatever number *n* happens to be. That is, you choose to let your subsequent desires, decisions and actions unfold according to lineage *n*. What, then, is your choice? Well, it's something that exists or occurs, and so, according to determinism, has a cause that makes it inevitable. And this cause, in turn, has a further cause and so on. The point is that your choice to follow one causal lineage rather than another is *itself* something that is part of a causal lineage and so is no more free than anything else in a causal lineage. So, we cannot safeguard freedom by trying to locate in the choice between competing causal lineages, because any choice made between such lineages is itself part of a causal lineage, and so made inevitable by what has gone before it.

This is all a little abstract, and an example will help clear things up. Suppose you are Tom Cruise in that pivotal scene of the movie, confronting Leo Crow in the hotel room. Various causal lineages stretch out in front of you. One of these involves shooting Leo Crow, which you really want to do. Another involves arresting him, or letting him go, or turning yourself in to the Pre-Crime unit, or even killing yourself. These are all possible courses of action open to you. If determinism is true, then each of these possible causal lineages is the result of previous causes, which are themselves the result of even more previous causes. The suggestion is that human freedom lies in the ability to choose between these lineages. So, if Tom chooses to let Leo Crow go, rather than blow him away, this is a free choice on Tom's part. But a moment's thought should make us see that this isn't going to work. For Tom's choice is itself part of yet another causal lineage, and so is something made inevitable by the lineage of causes from which it derives. Whether Tom gives in to his urge and wastes Crow, or whether he lets him go, this choice is made inevitable by what has happened before. We can't find freedom in the choice between causal lineages, because that choice is part of a further causal lineage, and so raises the same problem all over again.

DETERMINISM AND PREDESTINATION

People often confuse determinism with what's known as *predestination*, so before we go on let's get the difference between the two straightened out. The views are, in fact, superficially similar, and so confusing them is a pretty natural thing to do.

First, determinism. Determinism claims, in effect, that what you now do (and choose and decide) is predetermined. You had to act and choose and decide in the way you did. You had no choice. Your choices, decisions and actions are inevitable – and they are made inevitable by what has gone on in the past. So what happens now, and what happens in the future, is inevitable.

Predestination, on the other hand, is the view that no matter what you do now – no matter what you choose and decide, and no matter how you act – the future is going to turn out the same. No matter whether you turn yourself in to the Pre-Crime unit or go on the run, if you are destined to shoot Leo Crow at a certain time, you will shoot him. What happens in the present is irrelevant to what happens in the future – for the future is fixed.

Do you see the difference? Determinism is the view that you have no choice over what you do now. Your actions, choices and decisions that you perform and make now are inevitable – you couldn't have done things any differently. So, according to determinism, the future is indeed fixed. But it is fixed because the present is fixed. And the present is fixed by what has gone on in the past. Predestination, on the other hand, presupposes that you could do things differently now – you have a choice over what you do now. It's just that this will make no difference to the future. So, the future, according to the predestination view, is fixed, but not fixed by the present and past. According to determinism, on the other hand, the future is fixed by the past and by the present (which, of course, is, relative to the future, the past).

the precogs and laplace's demon

The great seventeenth-century scientist Pierre Laplace was a determinist. He saw the universe as a gigantic and intricate mechanism, made up of many parts interacting with each other in complex but, in principle, predictable ways. Apparently, he was having a chat with Napoleon one day, when Le Petit Général asked him what role God played in his system. Laplace replied that he had no need of that hypothesis. The giant deterministic mechanism that Laplace envisaged the universe to be was incompatible with God's action on the world, because God's action would, presumably, be free, and there was no room for free action in Laplace's deterministic system.

According to Laplace, however, a hypothetical super-being like God would be able to predict the exact development of the universe. As long as He knew the initial state of the universe, it would be, in principle, possible to predict everything that was going to happen, at the exact time it was going to happen. This hypothetical super-being became known as *Laplace's demon*.

The precogs of *Minority Report* are, in effect, a sort of truncated Laplace's demon. They cannot predict everything that will happen, but they can predict murders. Notice that their ability is not based on predicting the motives or *intentions* of the murderers – Tom Cruise makes that very clear in an early and helpful explanation of their powers. Their ability is not based on predicting what you intend to do, but on seeing what you will actually do. Nor is their power based on calculation of probabilities. They are not supposed to be predicting the most likely outcomes of events – what has the highest probability of occurring. Rather, they are supposed to be seeing what will actually happen. Otherwise, the rationale for the Pre-Crime unit would be undermined. You can't go around sending a man off to indefinite suspended animation on the grounds that the most likely scenario was that he would murder his wife and her lover. For that, you need certainty not probability. And to be certain about a future event, that event must actually happen. How can this be? Well, since the future has not yet happened, it can only be if the future is made inevitable by what's going on in the present and what has gone on in the past. The present is fixed or determined by the past, and the future is fixed or determined by the present. And this is precisely what determinism claims. You can, legitimately, have a judicial system based on precogs, therefore, only if the future is fixed by the past and present. That is – if determinism is true.

There is, of course, a paradox involved here, one discussed, briefly and inadequately, in the film. If the precogs see the future, then Tom and the Pre-Crime unit spring into action, and the murder is (hopefully) prevented. But this means that the murder was destined not to happen after all. So, how could the precogs, whose ability is supposedly to see what actually happens, rather than predict what is most likely to happen, see something that wasn't, in fact, going to happen? They must be seeing something that wasn't fixed or determined at all. Which, of course, undermines the entire rationale for the Pre-Crime unit, and the judicial justification for putting into suspended animation those people who actually never got around to doing anything at all. Oh well, nothing's perfect.

INDETERMINISM

If determinism is true, then it is easy to see why there is a problem for the notion of free will. Everything that happens is inevitable – whatever happens had to happen in the way it did. And it is difficult to see how this leaves room for the idea of free choice and action. However, so far, you might not be particularly convinced or worried. One reason for your insouciance might be that you realise the determinist argument depends on an assumption, one that you do not share. The assumption is that everything that exists or occurs has a cause. Without this assumption, the determinist argument isn't even going to get off the ground. So, all we need to do to scupper the argument for determinism is reject the claim that everything that exists or occurs has a cause. This position is quite well known; it goes by various names but we will call it *indeterminism*.

This line of argument is a common one. And we often find it developed by way of a distinction between *cause* and *influence*. Here is where I am likely to be accused of over-simplifying again.

You might want to argue that whereas our actions may be *influenced* by preceding events, they are not *caused* by those preceding events, and so are not made inevitable by them. Our actions, choices and decisions may be influenced by all sorts of things, but this does not mean that they are made inevitable by them. So, hurray for human freedom and dignity again.

But what does this idea of *influence* amount to here? Suppose we said, for example, that the explosion was *influenced* by the occurrence of a spark. What would this mean? Well, one thing it could mean was that the spark was not the *total* cause of the explosion, that other things like the presence of oxygen are also necessary. Similarly, we might say that a desire was not the total cause of the action. This is all perfectly clear. But it does not get us around the problem of determinism. Because determinism is the view that everything that exists or occurs has a total cause, and so is made inevitable by what happens before it. The desire may not be the total cause of the action, but if the action does have a total cause, then the action is inevitable, and so, it seems, not free. So, vague talk of *influence* is not going to get us around the problem if all we mean by influence is *partial cause*.

The idea of actions being influenced rather than caused is going to help us only if we bite the bullet and distinguish influences from any sort of cause. That is, when we talk of influence, what we are pointing to is some sort of gap in the causal order – some sort of hiatus or hole in the labyrinth of causal lineages that make up the history of the universe. An action can be free, on this view, because it is not caused. And this is precisely what indeterminism claims. So, appealing to the notion of influence, when push comes to shove, is a way of claiming that actions are free precisely because they are not caused. So, it's hurray for human freedom and dignity again only if indeterminism turns out to provide us with a satisfactory account of that freedom and dignity.

Indeterminism, like its determinist adversary, is made up of two basic claims, the mirror images of the determinist claims. According to indeterminism:

1. at least some human actions, choices and decisions do not have causes;
2. those actions, choices and decisions that do not have causes are, therefore, free.

Indeterminists are not committed to the idea that *all* human actions, choices and decisions are free. They can allow that some of these things have causes, and when this happens, the action, choice or decision, the indeterminist says, will not be free. What the indeterminist says is that *at least some* human actions, choices and decisions do not have causes, and when this happens, the action, choice or decision is free: it is free precisely because it doesn't have a cause.

To those of you who think indeterminism rescues human freedom from the clutches of determinism, and who are not, therefore, worried by the argument for determinism, I say this: it's time to be worried, it's time to be very worried. Indeterminism cannot possibly work as an account of human freedom.

Suppose you were unfortunate enough to have a neurological condition that resulted in a pronounced nervous twitch. Suppose that every now and then your right arm shoots out horizontally from your side. You don't have any control over this, because you don't have any control over the neurological problem that causes it. So, you can be walking down the street, for example, minding your own business, when your arm shoots rapidly out to your side, hitting the nearest passer-by. Or you are out on a date, things are going very well, and you think you may just get lucky tonight, when, 'whack!', your arm shoots out and renders your date unconscious. Clearly you don't have any control over this, and so the action of your arm moving out from your side is not a free one.[1]

Now, in this case, the movement of your arm has a cause, an annoying neurological condition. And because you have no control over the cause, you have no control over the movement either. Now imagine a slightly different scenario. Your arm shoots out in the same way, but this time it *has no cause*. What makes the arm move? Nothing, it just does. That's what it means to say that it has no cause. Nothing makes it move – it moves *for no reason*. Now, if you're like me, you'll have a really hard time imagining this. But this is what the indeterminist requires us to imagine; for, according to the indeterminist, whenever a free action occurs, this is what it is like. The action is free when and only when it is not caused (or when it results from a decision or desire that is uncaused). Now, let's give the indeterminist the benefit of the doubt, and suppose that she has described a coherent or imaginable situation. The question is this: is an action that comes about in this way a free one?

---

1. Indeed, so not free is it, that most philosophers would not even regard it as an action, but just a bodily movement. For more on this see later.

I think, pretty clearly, that it is not. In fact, it is no more a free movement when your arm shoots out for no reason at all than it is when it shoots out as a result of the neurological condition. You have no control over the event in either case. In the first case, you have no control over your arm because it is made inevitable by something, the neurophysiological problem, over which you have no control. But in the second case, your arm just shoots out for no reason; the movement has no cause. But, then, you have no control over the movement. In order for you to have control over the movement of your arm, there must be some connection between you and the movement, you must have some say in whether your arm moves. That is, if the movement of your arm is to be a free movement, then it must be something that *you make happen*.

So, if the movement of your arm has no cause, and therefore happens for no reason, it cannot be something that you make happen. And, therefore, it cannot be a free movement: it is not a movement that is the result of your free will. What's gone wrong with indeterminism? Basically, the indeterminist has confused two very different things: *freedom* and *spontaneity*. If your arm moves for no reason at all, then this means only that the movement is spontaneous or *random*. But if it is to be genuinely free, the movement must be something that you make happen; it must be something that you bring about; it must be something that you *cause*.

The same sort of point applies when we switch from actions to choices and decisions. A choice or decision that came about for no reason at all would be a truly terrifying thing. You would have no role in bringing about that choice or decision, it would be something that simply happened, randomly, for no reason. You might wake up one morning full of the joys of spring, looking forward to whatever new adventures the day might bring, and then suddenly decide to kill yourself. Why? For no reason. No reason at all. This is what a decision that came about for no reason would be like. It would just suddenly be there, you have no idea why, and, indeed, there is no reason why. Free decisions are not like that. Free decisions must have some connection to other things you feel and think, they cannot come about for no reason. They must be something you have some say in. That is, deciding must be something that you *do* – something that you make happen – not merely something that happens to you.

At one time it was fashionable to try to find the solution to the problem of free will in quantum theory – the branch of physics that deals with the behaviour of subatomic entities. So, you would find people arguing like this. At the quantum level, some events occur for no reason, without any cause. Therefore, if this can occur at the quantum level, it might also be responsible for human free will. Now, this is almost certainly a misunderstanding of quantum theory anyway. But suppose it was not. The fact that events can occur without a cause shows only that they are random or spontaneous, not that they are free. So, even if it were possible to extend the findings of quantum theory to the issue of free will (and it is, in fact, possible for quantum effects to have large-scale ramifications), all this extension could give you would be the randomness or spontaneity of human action, not its freedom.

tHe DILemma of DetermInISm

This puts the believer in free will in a spot of bother. The trouble takes the form of what is known as a *dilemma*. You're probably familiar with the expression: *you're damned if you do, damned if you don't*. Well, this is what a dilemma is, really. In the free will case, the dilemma looks like this:

P1 If our actions, choices and decisions are caused then they are not free.

P2 If our actions, choices and decisions are not caused, they are still not free.

P3 Our actions, choices and decisions are either caused or they are not caused.

C Either way, our actions, choices and decisions are not free.

P1 is what determinists claim. Our actions, choices and decisions are caused, along with everything else that exists or occurs. Add to this the claim that causes make their effects inevitable, and we seem to arrive at the conclusion that our actions, choices and decisions are not free. They can't be because what happens inevitably happens. P2 stems from the failure of indeterminism. Actions, choices and decisions that are not caused or simply random or spontaneous. They are not free since you have no control over them. Either way, our actions and choices and decisions are not free. We're damned if they're caused, and we're damned if they are not. Causation robs us of our freedom, whether it applies to us or not. This is known as the *dilemma of determinism*.

Is there any way out of this dilemma? Is there any way of salvaging our freedom?

COMPATIBILISM

Determinism and indeterminism have one thing in common. They both assume that *causation is incompatible with freedom*. That is, they both assume that *if* an action, choice or decision is caused, then it cannot be free; its being caused is incompatible with its being free. For this reason, determinism and indeterminism are sometimes referred to as forms of *incompatibilism*. Freedom and causation are incompatible.

Many have thought that human freedom can be defended by questioning this assumption that is common to determinism and indeterminism. That is, many have argued that, in fact, the freedom of an action, choice or decision is perfectly compatible with its being caused, *as long as it is caused in the right sort of way*. This view, quite naturally, is known as *compatibilism*.

One of the most famous compatibilists was the Scottish philosopher David Hume (1711–76), who we met before in Chapter 2. According to Hume, the problem of freedom arises because people tend to confuse *causation* and *compulsion*. But this, according to Hume, is an illegitimate conflation of two very different things. There is a world of difference, for example, between my doing something because I want to do it, and doing it because someone has a gun to my head and will kill me if I don't. In the first case, in Hume's terminology, my action is caused, but in the second case it is compelled. According to compatibilists such as Hume, the opposite of freedom is compulsion, not causation. Therefore, they claim, my action is only not free if it is compelled. It can be caused and still be free as long as it is caused in the right sort of way.

If compatibilism is to succeed, then it will have to provide a viable account of what it means for an action to be caused *in the right sort of way* to make it free. Being caused to do something by a gun to my head is not the right sort of way, but doing that thing because I want to do it apparently is. On the basis of this sort of idea, compatibilists typically draw the distinction between free and unfree action by way of a distinction between *internal* and *external* causation. When I am forced to do something by a gun being put to my head, then, so the idea goes, this is causation by an external factor, the gun at my head. But when I do something because I want to, this is internal causation; my action is caused by an internal state of desiring or wanting. So, on the basis of this sort of idea, compatibilism is usually defined as follows:

- Actions, choices and decisions whose immediate cause is an internal state are free.
- Actions, choices and decisions whose immediate cause is an external state are not free.

In both cases, the actions, choices and decisions are caused. But in the second case, where the cause is external, the actions, choices and decisions are compelled. In the first case they are free, in the second case they are not. Is this going to work?

I don't think it is. First of all, there are serious problems with the compatibilist attempt to explain the freedom of an action in terms of the distinction between internal and external causation. The problems stem from the fact that *anything* that is going to count as an action must have an internal cause – including the compatibilist's standard examples of unfree actions. To see this, have a look at the following:

1. Leo Crow leaves the hotel room because he wants to confess his part in the plot to the Pre-Crime unit.

2. Leo leaves the hotel room because Tom puts a gun to his head and tells him to get out or else.

3. Leo leaves the hotel room because he is on the business end of Tom's 44 Magnum and hurtles out of the window.

Take (1). This is a case of an action that is clearly caused internally – by a desire of Leo's. So, no problem there – it's clearly a free action on the compatibilist story. How about case (2)? The compatibilist would tell us that this is a case of a compelled, and so unfree, action, because the cause is external – the gun to Leo's head. But is this right? The gun to Leo's head is not going to work, for example, if believes his life is worthless and that by dying he can secure a big payout for his family (which, in the film he, of course, did believe). The gun would work only if Leo has a desire to live. If so, then the immediate cause of his action would not be the gun but his desire. But this is an internal cause – and so the compatibilist would have to say that, in this case, Leo's action is free.

OK, you might say, but in the second version of events, we have not only an internal cause – Leo's desire to live – but also an external one – the gun to his head. And we do not have this in case (1), where the cause is simply Leo's desire to confess. And this is why the action is free in (1) but not in (2). But this doesn't seem to be true either. In (1), what makes Leo leave the hotel room is not only the internal state – his desire to confess – but also the external fact that the relevant members of the Pre-Crime unit are not there for him to confess to. In both cases, Leo's actions seem to stem from a complex combination of both internal *and* external factors.

Now consider case (3). Here, the factors that cause Leo to leave the hotel room are clearly external. But is leaving the hotel room, in this case, an *action* of Leo's? Pretty clearly, it isn't. Actions are things we *do*, but in case (3) we seem to be dealing not with something that Leo *does* but with something that *happens to* him. Leaving the hotel room, in the rather unfortunate way he left the hotel room in the film, is something that happens to him, not something he does. It's not an action at all, and so the issue of whether it is a free action simply does not arise. Leo doesn't do this freely, because he doesn't *do* it at all.

This is the problem for the compatibilist. Anything that has purely external causes is not an action at all, and so is irrelevant to the free will debate. But anything that does qualify as an action is the result of a combination of internal and external factors. Also, the most immediate cause of anything that is to count as an action is always an internal state – a desire to go to lunch, a desire to live and so on. So, the compatibilist cannot draw the distinction between free and unfree actions on the basis of the distinction between internal and external causation. Even if the compatibilist could iron out this problem, there are others. The compatibilist account of freedom basically amounts to this: *freedom is the ability to do as you please*. If you do what you want, then you are acting freely. But we have already seen what's wrong with this. Freedom must involve more than simply doing what you want. If your desire to read this book is not a freely chosen desire – but one hypnotically induced in you by unscrupulous marketing people – then you have no control over your having this desire. But if the desire, as cause of the action, makes the action inevitable, then neither do you have any control over your action of reading this book either. So, in order to have any control over your action, you also need to have control over the desire that produces it. In other words, genuine freedom involves more than doing as you please, it requires pleasing as you please too. Freedom is more than doing what you want – it is also having control over what you want. So, compatibilism can't be right.

agent causation theory

We are having a hard time explaining how we could possibly be free. Compatibilism seems to be a non-starter. So, freedom is incompatible with causation. But then, if our actions, choices and decisions are caused, they can't be free. And if they are not caused, they still can't be free – for then they would be merely random events over which we have no control. So, either way, we can't be free.

The final throw of the desperation dice for someone who wants to hang on to the idea that we are free is known as *agent causation theory*. This view starts from the plausible assumption that if an action, choice or decision is to be free then we must have control over it. And how do we have control over it? Basically, we make the action, choice or decision happen. So how do we explain this notion of *making* an action, choice or decision happen? According to agent causation theory, we can explain this in terms of the idea of causation by the *self* or *agent*. An action is a free action of yours when, and only when, *you* make it happen.

This is quite different from compatibilism. According to compatibilism, an action is free is if it is caused by a desire – an internal state – of you. According to agent causation theory, an action is free if it is produced by *you*, rather than one of your internal states. This might seem a small difference, but it's not. We understand, more or less, what is involved in an action being caused by a desire. But what is involved in an action being caused by you, as opposed to one of your desires? In particular, what is this *you* that causes your actions, choices and decisions?

And here lies the central problem for agent causation theories. We saw in the previous chapter that there are serious problems in making sense of the notion of a self as a substantial entity persisting through time. But if we can't do this, then we have no hope of making sense of the notion of actions being brought about by the self. We can develop this problem for agent causation theory in terms of the following question: Is this self that brings about our actions a physical thing or non-physical thing? The agent causation theorist, it seems, has three options.

1.   The self that causes our actions, choices and decisions is a physical thing.

2. The self that causes our actions, choices and decisions is a non-physical thing.

3. The self that causes our actions, choices and decisions is neither a physical nor non-physical thing.

(1) is not going to work. All physical things are firmly embedded in the causal order. And we explain the activity of physical things in terms of the activity of their parts. So, if the self were physical, we should be able to ask which parts of the self are responsible for which actions. Then, we would face the dilemma of determinism all over again. If the connection between a part of the self and an action is a causal one, then the action does not seem to be free. But if the connection is not causal, then it is still not free – it is now random or spontaneous, but not free. So, making the self a physical thing does not get us around the dilemma of determinism.

What if we make the self non-physical, as in option (2)? Well, then we are basically saddled with a version of dualism. And dualism is, as I said earlier, probably the most refuted view in the history of philosophy. Don't go there. And if you do decide to go there, then as we saw in Chapter 3, you're going to have the problem of explaining how this non-physical thing that the self is supposed to be could ever possibly have any effect on physical things like the body. And if it can't have any effect on physical things like the body, how can it possibly make the body act? A non-physical self cannot possibly explain *free* action, if it can't explain action at all.

The remaining option is to make the self neither physical nor non-physical. But what does this mean? What is this neither physical nor non-physical thing? And how does it causally interact with the physical body? As we saw in discussing the problems of dualism, causal interaction requires sharing of properties. Physical things, for example, can causally interact with each other only because they share relevant properties such as mass, velocity, momentum, kinetic energy. So, if this neither physical nor non-physical thing that the self is supposed to be is to affect a physical thing like the body – and it has to do this if we are to act in any way – then it must share certain relevant properties with this physical body. But what properties does this neither physical nor non-physical thing share with physical things? And if it shares enough properties to allow it to affect physical things causally, why does this not qualify it as a physical thing? The claim that the self is neither physical nor non-physical is horrendously obscure, and it is only its obscurity that tempts us into thinking there is anything worthwhile in this view. Cut it loose.

TOM CRUISE, LEO CROW AND THE IDEA OF HUMAN DIGNITY

In the pivotal scene of the entire movie, Tom Cruise is supposed to shoot Leo Crow. The shooting has been seen by the precogs, and there is no 'minority report' – a dissenting interpretation of events from one of the precogs. Therefore, Tom's shooting of Leo is inevitable. Or should be. Nevertheless, Agatha, whom Tom has kidnapped, is screaming at him that he is human and so has a choice. And, lo and behold, it appears he does. In a way. He chooses not to shoot Leo, thus striking a blow for human freedom and dignity. He has chosen not to kill Leo Crow, and his choice is, allegedly, free. And, from the inside, of course it is. What could be more obvious to Tom, and to everybody else, that we always have a choice, that we could always do other than we do.

But, from the outside, what the hell is this supposed to mean? Is there some gap in the causal order leading up to Tom's action, so that his action is not caused by his preceding decision or volition? Then his action is random or spontaneous, but it's not free. Is his volition – his act of will – not to shoot Crow something that is not causally determined by what's gone before? Then, again, it's random or spontaneous. But it's not free because it's not something that he makes happen, therefore not something over which he has any control. Is his action, or lack of action, free because it is caused in the right way – by his desire not to shoot Crow and thus prove his freedom, for example? But then his action is free only if he has control over his desire, and over the cause of his desire, and of the cause of the cause of his desire and so on. And eventually, of course, we find a cause of the cause ... over which Tom has no control. Therefore, ultimately Tom may be able to do as he pleases, but he can't please as he pleases. So, he can't be free. Is Tom's action or decision free because it is produced by *him*, as opposed to one of his desires? But what is this *him* that does the producing? If it is physical, then we are back with the problem of determinism. If it is non-physical, we are back with the multifarious problems of dualism. If it is neither physical nor non-physical, then we are taking refuge in obscurity. Either way, from the outside, the prospects for making sense of the idea that Tom is free are grim.

It is often supposed that human freedom is an essential precondition of what people sometimes refer to as human dignity.

I'm not sure what they mean by this – and I'm not sure that they're sure what they mean by this – but the idea that we are somehow privileged and special members of the universe seems to underlie this sort of talk. If this is what human dignity is supposed to mean, then I'm pretty sure we don't have it in the way those who want to believe we have it believe we have it. In the case of human freedom and dignity, I'm pretty sure that, from the inside, we want ourselves to have, and take ourselves as having, something that, from the outside, we can't possibly have. And we can't possibly have it because it's simply not there to be had.

As I said at the beginning of the chapter, this is about as big and bad-assed a problem as you can get in philosophy.

6 HOLLOW MAN
WHY BE MORAL?

THE RING OF GYGES

The Dutch Master, Paul Verhoeven, in addition to his seminal collaboration with Schwarzenegger on the problem of personal identity (see Chapter 4), is also responsible for *Hollow Man* (2000). This is an updated version of the (H.G. Wells inspired) *Invisible Man* series of films from the 1950s and '60s, revamped with a little of the trademark Verhoeven gore. Sadly, Verhoeven may be declining as a philosophical force. None of the bold originality of *Total Recall* is evident in this tale, nor do we find the sort of trenchant sociopolitical critique that dominated *Starship Troopers*. In fact, the film is a straightforward reworking of a story told by the ancient Greek philosopher Plato. The tale is known as 'The Ring of Gyges', and occurred in Plato's most famous work, *The Republic*.

Gyges is a shepherd in a place called Lydia. One day he's out with his flock when a violent earthquake opens up an underground cavern. Gyges ventures into this cavern and finds the body of a larger than life humanoid figure, and on its finger is a gold ring. Gyges, clearly a shepherd not averse to a little grave-robbing on the side, rips the ring off the finger, and heads off back to his flock. Later that night, while hanging out with his fellow shepherds, he happens to turn the collet of the ring inwards, and he immediately turns invisible. His fellow shepherds, who don't seem to notice that he has suddenly vanished, start talking about him as if he's not there, which, as far as they are concerned, he is not. When he turns the collet of the ring outwards, he becomes visible again. Gyges, realising that he has totally lucked out, heads off to the big city, where he (1) shags the queen, (2) murders the king, (3) takes over the country and (4) becomes the progenitor of a long line of rulers of Lydia, including the well-known Croesus.

Now, no one can say the boy ain't done good. In one sense of *good* anyway. A humble shepherd rising to the station of king, and exchanging lonely nights out on the mountain, his sheep his only companions, for the comforts of the queen's boudoir and control of a kingdom. But, if, in one sense, he has done good, is there any sense in which he has done *bad*? This is the question Plato is concerned with. Plato, being (mostly) sane, intended this tale as allegorical rather than factual, and he uses it to throw into sharp relief the fundamental question of moral philosophy: *why be moral*? If you had the ring of Gyges, Plato asks, should you bother being *moral*? Is there any reason not to be a total bastard once the possibility of discovery and sanction have been taken away?

For example, let's suppose that Gyges, prior to his discovery of the ring, gets a little lonely out there on the mountain. Night after night, with nothing to do except tend to his flock. So, one night he thinks, 'Oh well, I might as well shag a sheep or two.'

Unfortunately, he picks the night when the shepherds from the surrounding mountains decide to pay him a visit, and there he is, caught *in flagrante delicto*, with sheep number 423 (or 'Buffy', as he likes to call her). His excuse – 'Buffy was stuck in a hedge, and I was just trying to help her through, honestly …' – fails, not entirely unexpectedly, to convince his colleagues, and he then becomes the subject of the sort of ridicule, derision and opprobrium reserved for sheep-shaggers or, rather, since all his colleagues were probably doing it anyway, sheep-shaggers who get *caught*.

Just think how different things might have been if only he had found the invisibility ring sooner. What would the ring have brought him? Essentially, the possibility of acting without consequences. Of doing what he wanted without the inevitable sanctions that usually follow. Of looking good, even when he wasn't being good. And, when he was being bad, of not looking anything at all. In such circumstances, would there have been anything wrong with Gyges shagging Buffy? And there we have it, the fundamental question of morality. Not exactly as Plato would have put it, perhaps, but you get the picture.

HOLLOW MAN

Hollow Man (Verhoeven, 2000) is essentially a retelling of 'The Ring of Gyges'. Kevin Bacon is a scientist and a bit of a bastard really. He's also brilliant, and, along with Elizabeth Shue, has been working for years on a way of making things invisible. While having success with animals, the procedure has yet to succeed with anything as large as a gorilla. Faced with removal of his funding, he applies the procedure to himself, as we all knew he would, and it succeeds. The only hitch is that he is unable to make himself visible again. So his colleagues make him up a scary moulded rubber mask, and confine him to the lab. Our Kev, however, is understandably unhappy about being cooped up in the lab when the world has so many inviting possibilities for an invisible man. So he absconds, and goes around doing various naughty things, of progressively increasing naughtiness. It begins with spying on a few naked women, progressing through the sexual assault of Elizabeth Shue (his ex-girlfriend), killing the boss of the research facility, and eventually trying to kill all of his former co-workers (and nearly succeeding too). It's the old story. Kev plays a man who was bit of a bastard anyway, and then becomes a total bastard once the possibility of being discovered and punished is removed. Is there anything wrong with this?

WHY BE MORAL?

The question *Hollow Man* deals with is sometimes referred to as the *ultimate question*. Of course, it's really no such thing. But it's still a big one. The question is: *why be moral*? What does this mean? Well, we humans can have at least two sorts of reasons for doing something. One reason is that we *want* to. What reason did Kevin Bacon have for spying on naked women, and assaulting Elizabeth Shue? Well, basically, he wanted to. He was, broadly speaking, *interested* in these activities. It is this interest that provides his reason for acting in the way he did. He also has longer-term interests – keeping his secret of invisibility safe from the powers that be, for example. Why does he have this interest? Because safeguarding this interest is necessary for him to keep enjoying the things he likes doing – and more generally throwing his weight around without having to suffer any sanction or punishment from society. These sorts of reasons for acting, we can call *prudential reasons*. We have prudential reasons because we have interests, and we have interests because we have desires. Our prudential reasons, therefore, are a function of what we *want*.

However, we can also act for what appears to be a different type of reason. We can sometimes do something because we believe – rightly or wrongly – that it is the *right* thing to do. Not necessarily 'right' for us, at least not in any prudential sense, but *morally* right. Indeed, often what we believe is morally right does not coincide with what we want, and so does not coincide with our prudential reasons for acting at all. If Kevin Bacon was not such a bastard to begin with, then he might have hesitated in attempting to rape Elizabeth Shue and kill all his co-workers on the grounds that these actions would have been morally wrong. And this would be true no matter how much he presently wanted to rape Ms Shue, and no matter how much offing his co-workers would be in his long-term interests. When we do something because we believe that it is the right thing to do, and when we refrain from doing something because we believe it is the wrong thing to do, we are acting from what we can call *moral reasons*.

Our question, then, becomes this: *why act from moral reasons rather than prudential reasons?* In any situation where moral reasons and prudential reasons conflict – and it appears they often do – why allow the moral reasons to outweigh the prudential reasons? This is the fundamental question – the ultimate question – of morality.

GOD IS WATCHING US

If we believe in God, there's no problem. God is watching us. Even if we are invisible men or women, God can still see us. More than that, if we behave like Kevin Bacon, then great is going to be His wrath, and He shall smite us, or something like that.

Appealing to God basically transforms moral reasons into prudential ones. Moral reasons are just one species of prudential reasons. It is in our own long-term interests to act morally because if we don't God is going to send us to Hell, where fiends will stick red-hot pitchforks up our bottoms, and stuff like that. None of us, presumably, would want red-hot pitchforks stuck up our bottoms, and so we have a very good reason to be moral – and this is a *prudential* reason to be moral. Hell being what it is, it is in our long-term interests to behave morally.

People who believe this is the only reason to be moral genuinely scare me. What would happen to them if they, for some reason, found they no longer believed in God? To tie moral behaviour so closely to the possibility of punishment is a sociopath's view of morality. But this aside, the increasing secularisation of society does leave us with a something of a problem. If there is no God, then we cannot collapse moral reasons into prudential reasons in this way. So what reason do we have for acting morally? What reasons do we have for allowing moral reasons to override prudential ones? Are we not implicitly holding on to an objective and binding God-made moral law, while rejecting the God who made it?

One way of answering this question involves, basically, replacing God with society.

nasty, brutish, and short

Not a description of Harvey Keitel, but an epithet applied by the fifteenth-century English philosopher Thomas Hobbes to describe the life of humans in what he called a 'state of nature'. This idea, and the resulting view of morality, provides one way of answering the question 'why be moral?' According to Hobbes, human beings are all, essentially, *egoists*. That is, we are nasty, vicious, acquisitive and, above all, self-interested little scumbags who would willingly sell our grannies for sex. We are all out for what we can get, and we want as much of this as possible, and we will do pretty much whatever we can to get it. So, the fundamental rule of life is: *do whatever you can to get whatever you want*.

However, things are more complicated than this. Because while you are doing whatever you can to get whatever you want, so too is everyone else. You are an egoist, but so too is everyone else. You may want to have sex with Elizabeth Shue, but Ms Shue is almost certainly none too keen on the idea, and if you take steps to force yourself on her, she, in turn, is likely to take steps to force certain consequences on you. You may want to kill all your co-workers in your research facility, but if you try to follow up on this, they are likely to react with extreme prejudice. More generally, if you do bad things to other people, they are likely to try and do the same to you.

And this, of course, is a risky business. As Hobbes said, a situation of this sort would be a struggle of each against all, and a life in this situation would be 'solitary, poor, nasty, brutish, and short'. How much more sensible it would be if we struck various agreements with other people. You don't try to kill me, and I t try to kill you. You don't try to rape me, and I won't send my brothers around with pipe cutters and a blowtorch. In others words, how much more sensible it would be if you formed a sort of *contract* with other people, a contract that placed certain restrictions on your freedom in return for certain restrictions on theirs. This idea provides the basis for so-called *social contract* theories of morality.

The idea is that while we are all, necessarily, egoists, we can be egoists of two sorts: stupid or rational. All egoists are out for what they can get, but rational ones are a lot cleverer about it than stupid ones. In particular, rational ones realise that what they want can be got a lot more easily if they cooperate with other people. The most basic needs of people – security, food, shelter, etc. – can be obtained most easily by cooperating with other people: agreeing to certain restrictions on your freedom if they will, likewise, accept certain restrictions on theirs. You scratch my back, I'll scratch yours, sort of thing. The result is that there is a sort of implicit contract, a social contract, governing the actions of rational egoists. If you are a stupid egoist, and simply try to get whatever you want by what-ever means possible, then the chances are you will not do – or sur-vive – anywhere near as well as the rational egoist whose getting what he wants is based on cooperation with other people. Why? Because all the other *cooperating* rational egoists will quickly get together and 'sort you out'. So, even given that we are all selfish, acquisitive and vicious souls, our needs can best be satisfied within, rather than outside, the bounds of the social contract.

And so we arrive at the basic idea of social contract views of morality. It is morally right to obey the conditions of the contract.

Any action that falls within the contract is thus a right or just one. Any action that transgresses the conditions of the contract is morally wrong.

The idea of the social contract is not supposed to be a description of any actual historical situation. It is not as if people who were living solitary, poor, nasty, brutish and short lives decided to get together and hammer out a contract. I mean, how would they even get in a contractual situation – a situation where they were actually sitting down and hammering out a contract? Such a situation, for example, would be an ideal opportunity to eliminate some of your more dangerous adversaries. So, why not do that? In order for the contractual situation to be stable enough to facilitate hammering out a contract, it seems that we would already need a contract – a pre-contractual agreement that speci-fied how we were to behave in the contractual situation. But how would we get such a pre-contractual agreement for the contrac-tual situation? It seems that we would need pre-pre-contractual discussions to hammer out the pre-contractual agreement for the contractual situation. But, again, such discussions would provide an ideal opportunity to eliminate some of your adversaries. So we would need a contract to regulate how we were to behave in the pre-pre-contractual discussions. And so on. This is an example of what philosophers call an *infinite regress*.

So, as a description of some supposed historical situation, the social contract idea is a non-starter. But this is not how the idea works anyway. The idea is that the contract is not an *actual* but a *hypothetical* agreement. It is not as if anyone at any time ever actu-ally agreed to the contract, but, rather, that by virtue of simply living in an ordered society we have all implicitly bought into a contract. And the contract is simply the set of rules that a random group of rational egoists would agree to as promoting the maximal satisfaction of their desires or goals.

Why be moral? According to the social contract theory, this question is equivalent to 'Why obey the conditions of the contract?' And the answer provided by the social contract theory is that if you do not obey the conditions of the contract, you will be punished. Simple as that. The retributive role of God has been taken over by society.

HOLLOW MORALITY

What would the social contract theory say about Kevin Bacon? Or Gyges the sheep enthusiast for that matter? If Kevin Bacon attempts to kill all his co-workers, is he doing anything wrong according to the social contract theory? The thing about the invisibility gig is that the possibility of sanction has, for all intents and purposes, been removed. If you should be moral because of the threat of sanction from other people, then why should you be moral if there is no threat of sanction? The answer with which the social contract theory provides us is, it seems: *you shouldn't bother*.

This is indicative of a general problem with the social contract theory. The whole point of contracting with other people – accepting certain restrictions on your freedom in return for similar restrictions on theirs – is to further your own interests. But advancing your own interests by way of this sort of cooperation with others makes sense only if one of two conditions holds.

1. First, others are a *threat*, or potential threat, to you. If they were not a threat or at least a potential threat, then they cannot provide a risk to the satisfying of your interests. So there's no point contracting with them.

2. Secondly, the others are a help, or potential help, to you. If they can provide you with no help, at least potentially, in the furthering of your own interests, there wouldn't be any point in contracting with them either.

The whole point of contracting with others, according to the social contract theory, is to advance your own interests. But these can be advanced by other people only if those people are either a potential threat or a potential help to you. So there's no point in contracting with anyone else. But according to the social contract theory, the social contract defines the scope and limits of morality. It is right, morally right, to obey the rules of the contract, and wrong, morally wrong, to transgress those rules. So your moral obligations begin and end with the rules of the contract. And this means that you have no obligations to anyone or anything that does not fall within the scope of the contract. And this means, ultimately, that you have no moral obligations to anyone who is not a threat to you, or not a help to you, or both. Such people, for you, lie outside the scope of morality. No matter what you do to them, your treatment of them cannot, by definition, be morally wrong (or morally right for that matter).

Just think of all the human beings who fall outside the scope of social contract morality. These include: infants, children, the senile, the mentally disadvantaged, the physically disadvantaged. People such as these typically get into the contract indirectly, by proxy, as it were. Babies, for example, typically have parents and extended family that will make life extremely unpleasant for you if you mess with their babies. But this is not always the case. You and a pregnant woman are shipwrecked on a desert island. The pregnant woman dies in childbirth, but the baby survives. Would it be morally legitimate for you to do anything you like to the baby, simply because there is no one there to protect it and get it into the contract by proxy? This flies in the face of everything we believe about morality. Yet the social contract theory seems to entail that everything that can neither threaten nor further your goals – directly or indirectly – is outside the scope of your moral universe. You have no moral obligations to such a person, and your treatment of that person can be neither morally right nor wrong – no matter what you do.

Social contract morality is a *hollow* morality. Kevin Bacon's transition to invisibility drastically alters the class of people who might be a help or a hindrance to him, and to the furthering of his interests. These people – notably Elizabeth Shue and the rest of his co-workers – now, according to the social contract theory, fall outside the scope of morality; at least they fall outside the scope of Kev's moral obligations. So, in trying to kill them, Kevin Bacon is doing nothing wrong. This view of morality is, I think, as hollow as the film's eponymous villain. Just like its religiously inspired precursor, the social contract theory ties the possibility of moral action too closely to the possibility of sanction or punishment – this time that of society rather than God. The idea that we should act morally only because of the possibility of societal punishment sanction is, again, a psychopath's view of morality.

can't we all just get along?

So, we're still in need of an answer to our question, 'Why be moral?' That is, why should we allow moral reasons to outweigh or override prudential ones? One tradition in moral philosophy, associated with our old friend, the Scottish philosopher David Hume, emphasises that the picture of human beings implicated in more simplistic versions of the social contract theory – the idea that we are all nasty, vicious, acquisitive and self-interested little scumbags who would willingly sell our grannies for sex – is not entirely accurate. Most of us wouldn't sell our grannies for sex at all – even if there were a geriatric Robert Redford indecently proposing to give us $1,000,000 for one night with her. Some of us like our grandmothers. Some of us like each other. Some of us are … *nice*.

So, as Hume and others have pointed out, we're not all like invisible Kevin Bacons. Some of us actually like our co-workers and friends, we are happy when we see them, and miss them when we don't. Some of us like doing nice things for other people. We're not all total bastards. And this raises the possibility that we might act on moral reasons rather than nakedly prudential ones because of these general feelings of fondness, affection, empathy, sympathy, fellow-feeling that we have for our friends and associates, and even for complete strangers.

I think there's a lot of truth in this. Of course, how much fondness, affection, empathy, sympathy, fellow-feeling you find is going to vary from person to person – the milk of human kindness has not been poured equally into every soul. But significant amounts of it are to be found in a lot of people. So, often, we may allow our beliefs about what's morally right to outweigh our prudential reasons because we are, basically, OK people. Does this enable us to answer our question, 'Why be moral?'

Unfortunately, it doesn't. What the question requires as an answer is, basically, some kind of *justification* for preferring moral reasons over prudential ones. That is, in order to answer the question, we need a *reason* for allowing moral reasons to outweigh prudential ones. What Hume's story provides us with is not a justification but simply a *causal explanation*. What's the difference? Well, suppose you say something outrageous, like, 'Sheep number 423 is looking rather ravishing tonight.' Your shocked companion exclaims, 'How can you say that!' You reply: 'It's easy, I open my mouth and the words come out.' What they wanted was a justification for what you said (since, clearly, 423 is not a patch on 271). But what you gave them was a causal explanation.

The Hume story amounts to this. Sometimes – basically because we like each other – we allow moral reasons to outweigh prudential reasons. This is simply what we do – as when we open our mouths and the words come out. But this is not a justification for allowing moral reasons to override prudential ones. But why do we need a justification? Because we need some sort of ammo with which to berate a rampant and invisible Kevin Bacon. We want to try and show that he *should* act morally, even if he doesn't have to. And to prove this, we need a justification for acting morally, for allowing moral reasons to trump prudential ones. We need to show that moral reasons *should* outweigh prudential ones. We cannot simply rely on the claim – even if it's true – that sometimes, in some people, they do.

Kant meets the invisible man

Another way of answering the question 'Why be moral?' is provided by the eighteenth-century German philosopher Immanuel Kant, whose answer is, in essence, simple: *consistency*. If you are immoral then you are, ultimately, *inconsistent*. Immorality reduces to inconsistency.

The strategy of both religious-based and social contract answers to the question 'Why be moral?' lies in trying to reduce moral reasons to prudential ones. So, when we say that you *ought* – morally – to do something, this ultimately reduces to the claim that you *ought* – prudentially – to do that thing. Doing whatever it is you ought to do is in your – short- or long-term – interests, and this is why you ought to do it. The genius of Kant was to see that there is another sense of *ought* – a logical or rational sense. In this sense, if you believe that Paul Verhoeven directed the film *Hollow Man*, then you ought, logically, to believe that Paul Verhoeven directed at least one film. If you believe the first without believing the second then you are being inconsistent, *logically* inconsistent. And so the idea of logical consistency provides us with a third sense of 'ought', in addition to moral and prudential senses. If you believe X, then you *ought*, logically, to believe everything that is entailed by X. In Kant, what we find, in all essentials, is the attempt to reduce the moral *ought* not to a prudential *ought*, but to a logical *ought*.

According to Kant, a good action – a morally right action – is always one that is done with a good *will* – and by 'will' he basically means 'motive' or 'intention'. In philosophy, there is an industry term used to apply to this position: Kant's view is said to be a *deontological* moral theory. A deontological moral theory is one that sees moral rightness or wrongness as being tied, at least in part, to the motives or intentions of the person who performs the action. The status of the action as morally right or wrong is tied, partly but essentially, to the status of the motive or intention that lies behind the action. In this, deontological views are opposed to what are known as *consequentialist* views, where the moral rightness or wrongness of an action is seen as being determined or fixed solely by the consequences of an action. According to consequentialism, the moral status of an action is determined solely by the consequences of the action, and has nothing to do with the motive with which a person performs that action.

So Kant was a deontologist in this sense. An action is a good one, morally speaking, if it is done, or performed, with a good motive. Of course, this doesn't help us at all unless we know what a good motive is. Kant's answer is that a good motive is one that turns on fulfilling one's *duty*. So, an action is good if it is performed with the motive or intention of fulfilling your duty. You act in the way you do because you want to fulfil your duty. And this, according to Kant, is the *only* thing that can make an action good.

This is not going to help us very much unless we know what our duty is. And different people, of course, have very different ideas on what their duty is. Just ask your local member of Al-Qaida. So, how do we work out what our duty is?

According to Kant, our fundamental duty is to obey what he called the *Categorical Imperative*: 'I ought never to act except in such a way that I can also will that my maxim should become a universal law.' Not exactly clear, admittedly – nothing Kant said ever really is. But what he's getting at is that morally correct actions – one's done from duty – have a sort of logical consistency that morally incorrect actions do not.

Take, for example, a policy of breaking your promises whenever it serves your own interests – an example of a triumph of prudential reasons over moral ones. A policy or rule of action is what Kant refers to by the term 'maxim' in the above quotation. Kant argues that you could never will that a maxim of breaking your promises whenever it suits you could become a universal law. What does 'universal law' mean? Basically, it's a law or rule that's adopted by everyone. A policy of lying, whenever it suited you, could not be consistently adopted by everyone. To see why not, ask yourself, 'What would happen if everyone broke promises whenever it suited them?'

First of all, if promises were routinely broken, then the whole activity of promising would become worthless. 'Yeah, right' would be the natural response to any supposed promise. But if promising became worthless in this sense, then people would soon stop making promises – there would simply be no point in doing so. But if no promises were made, then no promises could be broken – for the simple reason that there would be no promises there to be broken. So, the policy of breaking promises whenever it suits you could not be consistently adopted by everyone: you could not will, as Kant puts it, that this policy become a universal law. The policy of breaking promises is peculiarly self-undermining. If everyone routinely broke promises, soon no promises would be made, and so no promises could be broken.

The policy, in other words, is an *inconsistent* one. Therefore, breaking promises is morally wrong.

Don't misunderstand Kant here. He is not saying that breaking promises is wrong because it causes us a lot of trouble. That's the sort of thing a consequentialist would say. Nor is Kant saying that *if* you want to get on with other people you should keep your promises to them. There is nothing *iffy* about morality in Kant's view. Moral statements never have the form 'If you want X, then do/don't do Y' – for example, 'If you want to get on with your neighbour, don't have sex with his wife.' That's the sort of thing the social contract theorist would say. Rather morality, for Kant, is always categorical in form. 'Thou shalt do this', 'Thou shalt not do that.'

What Kant is claiming is that breaking promises is wrong because it is an inconsistent policy – it cannot be consistently adopted by everyone. And so you cannot consistently will that it become a universal law. Therefore, we arrive at Kant's criterion for distinguishing moral from immoral rules for action. Actions are morally wrong if the rules ('maxims') behind them cannot consistently be adopted by everyone. Moral wrongness, therefore, ultimately reduces to a form of logical inconsistency.

So to the question 'Why be moral?' Kant's answer is a simple one. If you are not moral, then you are being inconsistent. Simple as that. Is this idea going to work?

As we shall see more fully in Chapter 7, I think it's true that the notion of consistency is a big part of morality. One way of showing that someone's moral notions are misguided is by showing that they are inconsistent. But I think it very unlikely that consistency is all there is to morality. Besides, we are trying to work out an answer to the question, 'Why be moral?' And I don't think Kant's view answers this question.

To see why, let's look more closely at our question, 'Why be moral?' Actually, the question is ambiguous, and can be interpreted in at least two different ways: (1) Why should *I* be moral? (2) Why should *people in general* be moral? It might be true, for example, that *if* people in general were all to break their promises whenever they felt like it, then the practice of making promises would soon be abandoned, which would leave no promises to be broken. And so the general policy of breaking promises would be self-undermining, thus inconsistent. And this may be a reason why people in general should not break their promises whenever it suits them. But how is it an argument that *I* should not break my promises whenever it suits me? The policy of *my* breaking *my* promises whenever it suits *me* is not a self-undermining or inconsistent policy even if the policy of *everyone* breaking *their* promises whenever it suits *them* is. So Kant's argument can only show that the policy of everyone breaking their promises whenever it suits them is a morally bad policy. It would not show that my policy of breaking my promises whenever it suits me is a morally bad policy.

So, it's very unlikely that we can answer the question, 'Why should *I* be moral?' by appealing to the idea of consistency. Policies that may be inconsistent if everyone were to adopt them certainly need not be inconsistent if *I alone* adopt them. So we can't, I think, answer the question, 'Why should I be moral?' by attempting to understand 'should' as a logical 'should'.

WHAT DOES YOUR CONSCIENCE SAY?

The question 'Why should I be moral?' asks, in effect, for a reason to allow your behaviour to be bound or constrained by moral reasons at the expense of prudential reasons – considerations about what is morally right at the expense of considerations about what is best for me. You are faced with a choice – between having sex with Buffy the sheep or not, assaulting Elizabeth Shue or not, killing your co-workers or not. All of these, in principle, might be in your self-interest, assuming you are the sort of person warped enough to have interests of these sorts. So the question 'Why should I be moral?' amounts to the question of why you should let moral considerations override your interest in comely sheep, in comely research scientists, and in eradicating dangerous peers. What the question seems to require for an answer is a reason for preferring moral reasons over reasons of self-interest. And maybe this sort of question is not the sort of thing that can be answered.

To begin with, of course, the reasons for preferring moral reasons over reasons of self-interest cannot themselves be *moral* reasons. For the whole point of the question is why let moral reasons override reasons of self-interest. If we answered the question by appealing to moral reasons, then we wouldn't be answering the question at all. We would be *assuming* that moral reasons have overriding status, not providing a reason for why they should. But, almost as obviously, neither can the reasons we provide to answer the question be reasons of self-interest. For the question is one concerning whether reasons of morality outweigh reasons of self-interest, or vice versa. So appealing to reasons of self-interest would not answer the question, but beg that question. We would simply be assuming that reasons of self-interest outweigh moral reasons, not providing reasons for why they should.

And this is the problem. The question 'Why should I be moral?' seems to require for its answer reasons for why we *should* prefer one type of reason over another – moral reasons over reasons of self-interest, or vice versa. But it seems that we recognise three types of *should*. There is a moral 'should', as when you say you should do something, even if you don't want to do it, because it is the right thing to do. But we can't use this notion of should in answering the question, because that would presuppose that moral reasons win out over reasons of self-interest. There is another sense of 'should', a prudential sense, as when we say you should do something, even if you don't feel like it, because it's in your own long-term interests to do so. But we can't use this sense of 'should', because this is a prudential or self-interested sense, and this would presuppose that reasons of self-interest win out over moral reasons. Either way, we have not answered our question, we have simply begged it.

The problem is that we are running out of senses of 'should' with which to answer our question. There is, as we saw with Kant, another sense of 'should', a logical sense. We say, for example, that you should believe one thing given that you believe another because if you don't you are being inconsistent. If you believe that Kevin Bacon was better in *Tremors* than in *Hollow Man*, then you *should*, logically, believe that *Hollow Man* was not Kev's best role. If you don't, then you are, in some way, being logically inconsistent. And it was, as I said, Kant's genius to see that answering the question, 'Why should I be moral?' required a different sense of 'should' than either straightforward moral or prudential senses, and his task was, accordingly, to show that the moral could be reduced to the logical sense of should. However, as we have seen, it is very unlikely that Kant's efforts in this regard are going to work.

So we seem to have run out of senses of 'should'. So we can't answer the question. And the question is beginning to seem like the sort of thing that doesn't, indeed can't, have an answer. But, paradoxically enough, the fact that the question is not the sort of thing that can have an answer might be our best chance of answering it. I mean, you can't really beat yourself up over not being able to answer a question if that question, by its very nature, is not the sort of thing that can be answered.

Questions that don't have answers are very strange sorts of questions. Some say they are simply logically illegitimate in some way – pseudo-questions, little bits of nonsense that we have got into our heads. I don't agree, but such questions do, I think, show something quite profound about us and about the sorts of assumptions we are prone to making. There are certain questions that push us to the limits of reason. As the philosopher Ludwig Wittgenstein emphasised many times, all explanations have to come to an end somewhere. At some point, our reasons just give out. I think this is precisely the sort of question we are dealing with.

Often people tend to think that if you can't give a reason for a choice, then that choice is irrational. If this were true, then being moral would be an irrational choice. So, too would be being self-interested. But this assumption is misplaced. However, to say that something is not rational is not to say that it is irrational, it is to say that it is *arational*. Something is *arational* if it is simply not the sort of thing for which reasons can be sought or given. This does not make it irrational, it means, rather, that the question of its rationality or irrationality does not arise.

The choice to let one's life be guided by moral reasons or reasons of self-interest is, I think, ultimately an arational choice. The choice is ultimately one of self-definition: it is a choice guided not by reasons but by your image of the sort of person you want to be. Is this image not a reason? Not ultimately, because the desire to be a particular sort of person over another is not, itself, based on reasons.

One of Nietzsche's aphorisms runs something like this: 'What does your conscience say? You shall become what you are.' And choosing to live your life in a certain way, as one where moral considerations outweigh self-interested ones, or where self-interested reasons outweigh moral ones, or where both are constantly vying with each other to be top dog, is, in effect, a matter of becoming what you are. There may be no ultimate reason for being or becoming one sort of person rather than another. It is something we just do. It is our action – rather than our reason – that lies at the bottom of the self-definition game. The beginning of morality is the question 'Why be moral?' And in the beginning lies the *deed*.

7 INDEPENDENCE DAY & ALIENS
ᴛʜᴇ sᴄᴏᴘᴇ ᴏꜰ ᴍᴏʀᴀʟɪᴛy

ᴛʜᴇ ᴍᴏʀᴀʟ ɢᴀᴍᴇ

As we saw in the previous chapter, the choice of whether to be a moral creature, as opposed to an unashamedly self-interested one, is not a moral choice. It is not possible to give moral reasons, or a moral justification, for being a moral creature. Nor is it, ultimately, a rational choice either. At the end of the day, being moral is something we either do or don't do – it's not the sort of choice for which we can give reasons. It is our action that lies at the bottom of the moral game. But the choice to be moral is, in an important sense, a self-defining one – it runs to the core of the sort of person we are, and sort of person we aspire to be. Suppose we decide to define ourselves as moral creatures, what is involved in this?

If there are two (connected) themes that run through the moral game, in its various manifestations, they are these: *consistency* and *impartiality*. That's because our morality has been thoroughly dominated – some would say infected – with Christian morality. The fundamental rule of Christian moral thinking is the *golden* one: *do unto others as you would have them do to you*. Most moral theories, developed in the past few hundred years at least, are articulations of this general idea.

The basic idea behind the rule is something like this. Suppose you are considering doing something – say breaking a promise, killing a rival, or whatever. Then you should ask yourself, 'How would I like it if someone did that to me?' And if you decide you wouldn't like it, then you shouldn't do it. And it doesn't matter who it is that you imagine doing it to you. It's not as if you have to imagine your mate Bob breaking a promise to you or killing you. Anyone will do. And so we arrive at the idea that if an action is right for you to do, then it must be similarly right for anyone to do to you. It is this idea that is enshrined in the moral system developed by one of the most influential philosophers of all time – our old friend, Immanuel Kant.

KANT AGAIN

We've already come across the moral theory of Immanuel Kant. His central moral rule was what he called the *categorical imperative*: 'Act only on that maxim through which you can at the same time will that it should become a universal law.' You should tell the truth, for example, not because lying leads to a lot of unpleasant consequences (what consequentialists would say), nor because other people will not like you if you lie to them (the sort of thing social contract theorists would say), but because lying is an *inconsistent* policy – if everyone lies, soon no one promises things, or makes claims that other people are supposed to take as true, because there simply is no point. And since no truths are told, then no lies can be told either. So, lying whenever it suits you is a policy that undermines itself or cancels itself out. That, according to Kant, is why lying is wrong.

Kant's categorical imperative is, in essence, a jargonised version of the golden rule. What it says is that if an action is right for you to do, then it must also be right for everyone else to do. And if it is not right for everyone else to do, then it is not right for you to do. What this means is that if you are considering doing something, you should ask yourself, would it be possible for everyone to do this? And if it is not possible for everyone to do something consistently, then it is not right for you or anyone else to do it. So, this, then, is Kant's reinterpretation of the golden rule. First, moral rightness is to be understood in terms of the idea of *consistency*: if a policy cannot be consistently adopted by everyone, then it is a morally incorrect rule. Secondly, consistency is essentially connected with the idea of *impartiality*. A rule being consistently adopted involves the possibility of its equal adoption by everyone, no matter who they are. If a rule is right for you, then it must also be right for everyone else, no matter who they are.

The role played by impartiality is even more evident in one of Kant's alternative formulations of the categorical imperative. This formulation, although saying essentially the same thing, he calls by a different name – the *practical imperative*: 'Act in such a way that you always treat humanity whether in your own person or in the person of any other, never simply as a means but always at the same time as an end.' What does this mean?

Well, one thing is clear, according to Kant, we are supposed to treat every human being the same – as an *end*, and never simply as a *means*. What does it mean to treat them as a means? Well, first of all, what is a means? Basically, it is something that we use to further a goal or end. Medicine is a means to an end – the goal of getting better. Fast cars are a means to a further end – the goal of producing the thrilling sensation of speed, of impressing attractive members of the opposite sex, or whatever. Money is a means to a further end – of buying whatever it is you want to buy and so on. Bound up with the notion of a means is a claim concerning the sort of value possessed by means. A means has value to the extent, and only to the extent, that it helps you satisfy an end. Sometimes this is referred to as *instrumental* value – something has instrumental value if it has value only to the extent that it helps you get something else, whatever that something else may be.

So, to treat a person as a means is to treat them as a way – an instrument – of furthering your own goals, whatever those goals happen to be. And to treat them as a means *only* is to treat them as nothing more than a way of advancing your own goals. It is to treat them as a dupe, a stooge, a patsy, pawn, flunky, tool, lackey; as someone who is there to do things for you, and nothing more. And bound up with this is an implicit claim about the sort of value such a person possesses. If a person is a means only, then they have value only in so far as they can promote, or help you get, something that you want.

Humans, according to Kant, are not simply means. Each one of us, Kant claims, is an *end-in-itself*. Part of what he means by this is that we all have interests, goals, plans, purposes that do not reduce to, and are not a function of, the interests, goals, plans, purposes of anyone else. And part of the value each one of us has stems from the fact that we have interests, goals, plans and purposes of our own. This value is the value that we have independently of anyone else, and this is sometimes referred to as *intrinsic* or *inherent* value. So, according to Kant, we are not simply means, we are also ends, and so we possess more than instrumental value, we also possess intrinsic value.

So, according to the practical imperative, you should treat everyone – yourself included – not just as a means that has only instrumental value, but also as an end-in-itself that has intrinsic value. Some people, who didn't read Kant too well, thought that this precluded entering into any sort of commercial arrangement with anybody else. If I employ a plumber, for example, to unblock my drain, am I not treating him as a means to an end – my ends? Am I not treating him as if his value is a function of my interest in having a free-flowing sewage line? Yes, I am treating him as a means, but the point is that I am not treating him *simply* as a means. And there is nothing in the practical imperative that involves treating people as means, but only treating them *simply* as means, treating them as a means *only*. In employing a plumber, I don't treat him only as a means – as long as, for example, I *pay* him for his services. It's OK, according to Kant, to treat people as means, but, and this is crucial, not *only* as means.

The idea of impartiality is centrally involved in the practical imperative. *Everyone* is supposed to be treated as an end as well as a means. And this includes you as well as everyone else. For example, if you, like some people in unequal relationships, regarded yourself as having value only to the extent that you further the interests and goals of your partner, then you are not treating yourself as an end, but only as a means. And the practical imperative rules this out just as much as treating someone else as only a means. So, the pivotal idea underlying the practical imperative is *impartiality*. Everybody is to be treated with equal respect. Everyone, equally, is to be accorded the respect that goes with being an end-in-itself, as well as a means to other people's ends.

In this way, Kant builds a systematic moral edifice founded on the notions of consistency and impartiality. Morality is based on consistency in our dealings with other moral beings, and to be consistent requires impartiality – according each person the same respect they are due as an end-in-itself, and not merely a means.

the Greatest Good for the Greatest number

Another hugely influential way of developing the core concepts of consistency and impartiality lies in the moral theory known as *utilitarianism*, whose famous adherents include the eighteenth-century English philosopher Jeremy Bentham and the nineteenth-century English philosopher John Stuart Mill. In lots of ways, utilitarianism is very different from Kant's theory. Most importantly, utilitarianism is a form of *consequentialism*. That is, for utilitarianism, what determines whether an action is right or wrong are the consequences of that action, and only the consequences of that action. Nothing else. Kant, on the other hand, was a *deontologist*: the rightness or wrongness of an action is a function of the *maxim* behind the action – the motive or intention with which the action is performed. You've heard the saying,

'The road to hell is paved with good intentions.' Utilitarians would agree with this; Kant wouldn't have any of it.

Despite the huge difference between Kant's moral theory and that of the utilitarians, both find a central role for the notions of consistency and impartiality in moral reasoning. It's just that utilitarians have a rather different understanding of what impartiality amounts to. Most classical forms of utilitarianism start off with an assumption which is taken from the view known as *hedonism*: happiness is the ultimate good. Why believe this assumption? The basic idea is that happiness is the only thing that we seek for what it is in itself. All the other things we want – money, fast cars, big houses, companions – we want only because we believe these things will make us happy. We want happiness not because this is useful for some further goal or end we have; we want happiness for what it is in itself, not for anything else it can get us. So, hedonists argue that happiness is the ultimate good. That is, happiness, according to the hedonists, is the only thing that is intrinsically valuable. All other things have only instrumental value – if they are valuable it is only because they can help make you happy. This is the basic principle of hedonism, a view that originated with the ancient Greeks.

To this hedonistic idea, utilitarianism adds a social dimension. Indeed, utilitarianism is often referred to as a form of social hedonism. Suppose we accept that happiness is the ultimate good, the only thing that is intrinsically valuable. Then happiness is of primary importance. *Whose* happiness it is, and *when* that happiness occurs is of only secondary importance. Therefore, according to utilitarianism, we should attempt to produce or promote the maximum amount of happiness in the world. This should be our primary goal, and we should pay comparatively little attention to who it is that gets made happy and when they get made happy. The happiness of each person is no more and no less important than the happiness of any other person. So, the morally correct course of action in any given situation is one that produces the greatest overall amount of happiness. And this idea is summed up in a slogan associated with the utilitarian Jerry Bentham: *the greatest good for the greatest number*. Whenever we act, we should attempt to produce the greatest amount of happiness for the greatest number of people.

Once again, centrally implicated in the idea of utilitarianism is the idea of *impartiality*. Our actions should aim to produce the maximum amount of happiness, but whose happiness it is – whether it is mine rather than yours, or yours rather than mine – is irrelevant. That moral reasoning and decision-making should be impartial between people is, for utilitarianism, a consequence of the view that happiness is the overriding goal, and whose happiness it is is a relatively unimportant detail.

INDEPENDENCE DAY

Consistency and impartiality run to the very core of the way we think about morality. Therefore, perhaps it is not surprising that the role played by these concepts in moral reasoning has been the subject of a sizeable number of *sci-phi* films – one recent noticeable attempt being the 1996 Roland Emmerich blockbuster, *Independence Day*. In the eyes of many, this is a truly awful film, and the many in whose eyes the awfulness lies could back up their claim by citing, for example, the scene where the President's wife is dying, which, admittedly, still brings a substantial lump of bile to my throat. She had been dying for most of the film, after her helicopter crash left her with a perforated something or other, but still managed to drag herself halfway around the country inflicting her syrupy homilies on Will Smith's girlfriend and, by proxy, us. But the deathbed scene in the military hospital surpasses all this for sickly, cloying insincerity, and I think we could have all been legitimately spared it.

Nevertheless, we do have an interesting moral question here. Are the aliens doing anything wrong when they try to destroy us and ravage the planet? And trying to answer this is a good way of elucidating the role of consistency and impartiality in our moral reasoning. The same sorts of issues could have been discussed using Paul Verhoeven's truly excellent (1998) *Starship Troopers*. What a brilliant socio-political critique! The humans, all of them fascists to the core, are attacked by the previously peaceful inhabitants of Klendathu – the *bug planet*. It's the usual story of human imperialism, expanding into a domain of insects who basically like to keep themselves to themselves, and whose only real weapon against the human invaders seems to be farting – which admittedly is somehow strong enough to dislodge asteroids from their orbit and send them hurtling millions of light years towards Earth. Not a planet to visit if its inhabitants have been out on the beer. Who is right and who is wrong in this film? Who knows, but the same standards of consistency and impartiality would have to inform whatever evaluation we make.

Anyway, while I would love to talk about *Starship Troopers*, this would leave us with three chapters on Verhoeven – a straight-forward Verhoevenfest. So, the vastly inferior *Independence Day* it is.

Earth is invaded by a highly intelligent, yet morally suspect, species of aliens. The aliens wander the galaxy in huge space-going cities, themselves the size of small planets. Their lifestyle is that of sort of extraterrestrial Vikings. They wander the galaxy, and whenever they encounter a planet that might be of use to them, they rape and pillage it until there is nothing left. And if the dominant species on the plant in question objects, they eliminate that species. Then they move on. In this way, they move from planet to planet, taking and using whatever natural resources are useful to them from each planet they encounter. And, unfortunately, they've now arrived at Earth.

Still, they didn't count on the heroic American President, played heroically by Bill Pullman, nor the feisty USAF pilot, played feistily by Will Smith, nor the irritating computer genius, played irritatingly by Jeff Goldblum. And, basically, we win. Or, rather, America saves the world. Of course they do.

How to argue morally with aliens

The attitude of the aliens to the natural resources of the Earth, of course, brings to mind the attitudes of many humans to the Earth. The attitude is encapsulated in the slogan, currently doing the rounds in certain circles: *Earth First! We'll fuck up the other planets later.* The aliens, one might think, might have adopted a less consumerist lifestyle. Growth at any cost, they might have come to realise, is not all it's cracked up to be. But they didn't. Instead, they adopted the lifestyle of naked consumerism. Use up something until there's nothing left, then move on. Basically, this is what humans have been doing since we came down out of the trees. It's just that we have not yet become smart enough to export this strategy to other parts of the galaxy. There's that whole 'what is alien being held up as a mirror in which we can see ourselves more clearly' thing that is central to both sci-fi and *sci-phi*.

Anyway, I digress. Moving on, let's suppose that Bill Pullman, Will Smith and Jeff Goldblum decide to save the world by more subtle means. Instead of being President, Pilot and Computer Geek respectively, our triumvirate, let's suppose, are, in fact, a group of philosophers. And they are going to save the world by philosophical means? Curtains for humanity, you might think, and you would probably be right. Nevertheless, they're going to give it a go.

The reason they think they're got a chance is that extensive sociological studies of the aliens reveal them to have a moral system very much like ours. In particular, their sense of moral right and wrong, much like ours, is guided by the twin concepts of consistency and impartiality. The aliens believe that, in their moral dealings with one another, they are to abide by the idea of impartiality. Each alien is just as important as every other. All aliens, as they put it, are created equally.[1] That is, in their treatment of each other, at least when they are being moral, they are guided by an ideal of impartiality. Each alien must be accorded the same consideration and respect as any other. This is the seam our trio of heroes is going to exploit. They're going to use

---

1. Actually, they probably don't put it quite like this, of course, since they are unlikely to refer to themselves as 'aliens'.

the aliens' sense of moral justice against them. Sneaky human bastards.

The first thing to do is to work out why the aliens' moral thinking is governed by this idea of impartiality. The idea behind this principle is, basically, that:

> *Each alien should be treated with equal consideration and respect.*

This, we can call the alien *principle of impartiality*. What we want to work out is why they believe this principle. Did they have some sort of alien messiah, who bequeathed them a version of the *golden rule*? Actually, no. They are a much more logical species than us. And they realise exactly where their principle comes from – they understand, that is, the logical foundation of the principle of impartiality. We can call it the *principle of consistency*:

> *No moral difference without a relevant other difference.*

The aliens have realised that any system of morality based on the notions of consistency and impartiality – ours included – does not require a golden-rule-espousing messiah. Its justification is logical, rather than biblical. And it lies in the principle of no moral difference without some relevant other difference.

What does this principle mean? Well, consider two aliens, Worf and Schworf. Suppose Worf and Schworf are very similar. In fact, they have pretty much the same qualities and features. Both are honest, courageous and benevolent (at least by alien standards), and both have pretty much the same xenophobic/psychopathic attitude towards other life forms. In short, with regard to any features that might conceivably go into making a moral evaluation of them, Worf and Schworf are identical. Then, by the principle that there can be no moral difference without a relevant other difference, Worf and Schworf must be given the same moral evaluation. That is, either both must be good or neither is. Of course, which one of these evaluations is endorsed is likely to depend on whether you are human or alien. But the point is that even though humans and aliens might *disagree* on whether Worf and Schworf are good or not, nevertheless we both *agree* on the principle of consistency that underlies our moral judgments. Our moral judgments – judgments about who is good or bad, right or wrong – must be based on consideration of the relevant similarities and differences between people. So, given that both Worf and Schworf are the same in all their other relevant qualities, they must have the same moral qualities too. A difference in moral evaluation would be justifiable only if there is a relevant natural difference between the two, and, we are supposing, in our example there is not.

The same sorts of points apply to all other things that can be the subject of moral evaluation. Take actions, for example. If both Worf and Schworf help elderly female aliens across the road and assuming there is no relevant difference between their actions (e.g. both elderly female aliens want to cross the road etc.), if Worf's action is good, then Schworf's action must also be good. Conversely, if Worf's action is bad, so too must Schworf's action be bad.

We, and the aliens, morally evaluate many kinds of things: people, actions, rules, institutions. But in all cases, a difference in evaluation between two things of each kind – between two people, two actions or whatever – makes sense only if there is some other relevant difference between those two things. Where there is no relevant difference, so too can there be no legitimate difference in moral evaluation.

So far we have traced the alien commitment to impartiality to a more basic commitment to the principle of consistency – the idea that moral differences must rest on, or be derived from, a difference in other relevant features. Now, we have the aliens by the short and curlies, or by whatever passes for the short and curlies in aliens. All we have to do is show them that there are no relevant differences between them and us, between aliens and the human scum they plan to eradicate. Then they are going to be committed, on pain of inconsistency, to regarding us deserving of the same consideration and respect they accord each other. Easy as Sunday morning.

the alien response

There is, of course, a chance that it's not going to be easy as Sunday morning at all. The aliens might not be impressed with this move on our part – not one bit. Of course, they will accept that there can be no difference in moral evaluation without some relevant other difference. And so if each alien is accorded consideration and respect equal to that accorded every other alien, then humans must be given the same consideration and respect – unless there is some relevant difference between humans and aliens. But the problem (for us) is that the aliens are only too likely to think there are plenty of moral differences between us and them.

Intelligence is likely to figure first on the list of any alien respondent. Relative to them, we are really stupid creatures. They can build planet-sized spaceships and roam around the galaxy, whereas we haven't even managed the basic principles of warp drive, or whatever else it is that allows them to travel such distances. And this, they would argue, is the relevant difference that allows them to treat us like crap.

Can we get around this response? Is level of intelligence the morally relevant feature that the aliens have been looking for? Well, actually, I don't think so. The problem is that their suggestion falls victim to what is known as the *argument from marginal cases*. While it is true that *most* aliens are more intelligent than *most* humans, this is not true in all cases. First, some aliens, due to accidents at birth or misadventures on the part of the alien mother, are born with severe brain damage, resulting in equally severe retardation of their mental powers. Secondly, the intellectual powers of alien infants are not noticeably different from those of adult humans. Finally, many ageing aliens, through a variety of causes, suffer from a progressive deterioration in brain structure and function, and the intelligence of these aliens is certainly no greater, and in many cases less, than that of adult humans.

Therefore, if the aliens want to claim that humans can be treated like crap, or as we say in the business, lack *moral entitlements*, because of their inferior intelligence, then, if they are to be consistent, they must claim that these sorts of aliens also lack moral entitlements. So, whatever they do to humans can also legitimately be done to these sorts of aliens too. Happily for us – and for Pres, Top Gun and Geek who are philosophically protecting us – this flies in the face of the aliens' sense of justice. The aliens have a fairly strong moral sense, built up around the idea of impartiality, and this tells them that infant, brain-damaged and ageing aliens are just as entitled to respectful treatment as young and vibrant aliens at the height of their mental powers. And since they are also consistent creatures, they realise that they must drop intelligence as a candidate for the relevant difference between aliens and humans.

The same sort of problem is going to face most of the alien responses. To take just one more example, the aliens are telepathic, humans are not. Is this the big difference justifying their eradication of us? No, for there are various types of alien brain damage that can cause an alien to lose the ability to communicate telepathically, just as there are various types of human brain damage that can cause humans to lose the ability to communicate verbally. But few aliens – apart from some psychos – would want to claim that these unfortunate aliens – 'telepathically challenged' is, I think, the politically correct locution – are any less deserving of consideration and respect than more fortunate normal ones. So, the capacity for telepathy can't be the morally big difference.

The problem of marginal cases is a problem that undercuts most of the suggestions as to what might be the relevant difference between aliens and humans. Take a feature, almost any feature, that aliens typically have and humans don't have – an IQ of around 900, the ability to communicate telepathically, or whatever – and you will find that while most aliens have it, some do not. And so this feature could only provide a justification for the vile treatment aliens accord humans if the aliens were willing to hand out the same treatment to the unfortunate aliens in question. Given that they are not – for their treatment of other aliens is typically very good, at least in public – then they cannot use this feature as a justification for their genocidal inclinations towards humans.

There is, however, one feature that all aliens and only aliens have – the property of being an alien. By definition, every alien has this property, and no human does. So this feature is not vulnerable to the argument from marginal cases. Impressed by this fact, some aliens argue that this is the relevant difference that justifies their treatment of humans. Humans don't count morally, because they are not aliens. It's as simple as that. However, luckily for us, this suggestion also has serious problems. The difference between aliens and humans is ultimately a genetic difference. It's your genetic profile that determines to which species you belong. But the problem for the alien suggestion lies in explaining how a genetic difference, by itself, can be morally relevant.

To see this, let's first distinguish between genes and their effects. The effects of genes are what are known as *phenotypic* effects. The difference in intelligence between aliens and humans is, at least in part, the result of genetic differences between them and us. Level of intelligence is, therefore, in part, a phenotypic effect of a certain genotype, or genetic constitution. So too is telepathic ability and so on. Now it is easy to see how *some* of the *effects* of genes might be morally relevant. It's just that the ones we've looked at so far – intelligence and telepathic ability – are not. But here is a phenotypic effect that is almost certainly relevant: consciousness. For example, the difference between human and plant genotypes results in a difference in phenotypes, and this difference, it is easy to argue, gives humans a moral status completely different from that of plants. Crucially, humans have the ability to experience things, to suffer and enjoy, and consciously experience the world as being a certain way. Plants do not have this ability. This difference is usually accepted to be a morally relevant one: the capacity consciously to experience the world imparts a certain kind of moral status on creatures, a status that non-experiencing things cannot have. So, *some* – but as we have seen, not *all* – of the effects of genes can be morally relevant ones. But this does not mean that the genes themselves are morally relevant. Indeed, it is difficult to see how the positioning of certain molecules on an organic peptide chain can, by itself, be morally relevant.

It is never genes by themselves that are morally relevant, and genetic differences, by themselves, are not morally relevant differences. It is only what genes *do*, rather than what genes *are*, that can be morally relevant. That is, various genes can have phenotypic effects, and differences in the genes possessed by two creatures can result in phenotypic differences. So the question is not 'What are the genetic differences between aliens and humans?' For genetic differences, in themselves, are never going to be morally relevant. Rather, the question is, 'What phenotypic differences do the genetic differences between aliens and humans produce?' And then we should try to work out whether these phenotypic differences are morally different.

However, what are the major phenotypic differences between aliens and humans, the ones that may have a chance of turning out to be morally relevant? Both aliens and humans are conscious creatures – they both have the capacity to experience the world consciously and, on the basis of that ability, suffer or enjoy what happens to them. So there is no major phenotypic difference there. The major phenotypic differences seem, in fact, to be precisely the sorts of things we have already looked at – intelligence, telepathic ability, etc. And the suggestion that these are morally relevant can be undermined by the argument from marginal cases.

aliens R us

The alien invasion story of the sort typified by *Independence Day* is, of course, a thinly veiled moral parable, one that concerns our treatment of each other and of other creatures. Take three main 'isms' that have figured prominently in recent applied moral philosophy: racism, sexism and speciesism.

Take racism first. The sorts of arguments the aliens might use to justify their treatment of us are strongly reminiscent of the arguments used by racists to justify their treatment of other races. In all cases, racist arguments begin with the idea that there is some morally relevant difference between the favoured race, say whites, and some or other non-favoured race, say blacks. And this morally relevant difference justifies the favoured race's poor treatment of the non-favoured race. Implicit in this assumption, of course, is the idea that differential moral treatment of two things – in this case, races – is justifiable only if there is a morally relevant difference between these two things. That is, what underlies the argument is a tacit commitment to the principle of consistency.

The problem for the racist consists in trying to identify what this morally relevant difference might be. Like our alien would-be conquerors, intelligence has figured high on the list of racists. According to some racists, whites, say, deserve better treatment than blacks because they are more intelligent. The racist, of course, has the added disadvantage of his claim in this regard being almost certainly false – there are, in all likelihood, no innate differences in intelligence between different races. And so the racist is in an even weaker position than the alien – logically speaking. But even if the racist's claim of racially based differences in level of intelligence were true – which it is not – then this would still not help the racist. For he would still run slap bang into the argument from marginal cases. That is, even if it were true that whites were, on average, more intelligent than blacks, there would still be many below-average whites for whom this was not true. And then the white racist would, logically, be committed to treating those whites in the same way that he treats blacks.

The same sort of point can be made about sexism. In this case, the role of the aliens is typically played by males. That is, a male sexist will try to justify his inferior treatment of women by citing some morally relevant difference between males and females. Again, we have a tacit commitment to the principle of consistency underlying this. The problem for the sexist consists in trying to identify some morally relevant difference between men and women. Any proposed feature will almost certainly either turn out to be morally irrelevant (e.g. genetic differences), or will turn out to be undermined by the argument from marginal cases.

The parable of the alien invasion has what is probably its most obvious application to the issue of our treatment of other species. Here, we humans play the role of the aliens, and various animals play the role of the humans. Parallel to the racist and the sexist, we now have the *speciesist* – someone who thinks that members of other species are deserving of less consideration and respect simply because they are not human. Let's have a look at this idea in more detail, by way of another classic of the *sci-phi* genre, one that this book ignores at its peril: the series of films instigated by Ridley Scott's *Alien* (1979).

UICIOUS ALIENS?

We are first introduced to the eponymous villain of the films in 1979, when it lays an egg in a member of the crew (John Hurt) of a spaceship, and, in one of the most famous – and most spoofed – scenes of any sci-fi movie, bursts out of Hurt's chest leaving a rather nasty mess behind. Then in James (*The Terminator*) Cameron's *Aliens* (1986), Ripley, played in a career-defining way by Sigourney Weaver, the sole survivor of the original *Alien* encounter, is found floating in space after 57 years. She is sent with a group of marines to investigate the disappearance of a group of colonists from a remote planet. Bad move, because this time there's not one alien but thousands of them. There's plenty of blood and guts, and, of course, a hidden agenda supplied by the evil military-industrial complex that wants to explore the idea of using the aliens as weapons. There's also a good supporting role for Lance Henrikkson as the humanoid robot who, thanks to Arnie's efforts in Chapter 3, we can take seriously.

In the third film, *Alien*^{3} (1992), Ripley, again the only survivor of the previous film, finds herself (after she has been asleep in space again) on a penal planet, surrounded by nothing but horny men. And just when she thinks her luck is about to change, she discovers that (1) the aliens are around on this planet too, and (2) she was unknowingly 'impregnated' by an alien in the second film. She is carrying an alien larva inside her, one to which she 'gives birth' at the end of the film as she destroys herself by falling into a wall of fire.

Then finally (so far) in *Alien Resurrection*, Ripley is, *yet again*, the only survivor of the previous action. If you're an actor signed up to co-star with Sigourney Weaver in an *Alien* film, then I wouldn't go around making plans for a sequel. This time Sigourney plays not Ripley as such, but Ripley's clone, a clone that has some alien DNA inserted into her for good measure. Winona Ryder reprises the Lance Henrikkson role of *Aliens* as the robot that could show humans a thing or two about courage and decency. Again, it all ends pretty badly. Ripley escapes, this time with a few survivors – I wonder how many of them will meet an untimely end before *Alien 5*?

The aliens, of course, are portrayed as the baddies. And to be fair, they do have a rather nasty habit of laying their eggs in human bodies, which proves most inconvenient when the hatched creature bursts out of the chest of its human host. Very messy, and rather embarrassing if it should happen at, say, a dinner party. But are the aliens evil or simply misunderstood?

They are, after all, another species. So why should they have any moral obligations towards us? After all, we do terrible things to other species, far worse than the grossest alien excesses – just ask an intensively reared pig or chicken, or visit a slaughterhouse some time. At least they just kill us, and while this is a somewhat painful death, at least it happens suddenly and relatively quickly. In the name of cheap food, we inflict lives of untold misery and equally gruesome deaths on hundreds of millions of animals every year.

Surely I exaggerate! We can't compare human treatment of animals, even the ones we eat, to the wicked aliens' treatment of us. Can we? Yes, we can. In fact, compared to us, the aliens come across as a benign and gentle species. To see this, take an animal, one that we eat, any one will do. Take, for example, a chicken. Which would you prefer to be? A human gestating an alien larva, or an intensively reared chicken?

Suppose you are a chicken. First you are born. And that, I'm afraid, is about as good as it's going to get. If you are born a 'layer', but are male, then your flesh will be deemed not good enough for eating and your life will, accordingly, be short. If you are lucky, you will be gassed. If you're not so lucky, however, then you will be thrown into a plastic sack and allowed to suffocate under the weight of other chicks. Alternatively, you may simply be ground up while still alive.

If, on the other hand, you are a layer and female, your troubles are just beginning. First, probably when you are between one and ten days old, you will find yourself being *debeaked*. That is, a guillotine-like device with a red-hot blade will slice off your beak. Just be thankful you weren't born in the 1940s: then it would have been burned off with a blowtorch! But this won't hurt, will it? After all, aren't beaks simply horny outgrowths? Isn't it just like cutting nails, or something like that? Actually, no. Under the beak is a highly sensitive layer or soft tissue, infused with nerve endings. It's something like the layer of skin under the human nail. So, debeaking would be like trimming nails if your preferred method of doing so involved ripping through half your finger as well.

Following a second debeaking, you will be moved to a battery cage in a laying facility. If you are in the US, the cage will be approximately 12 by 20 inches; if you are in the EU it will be approximately 46 by 51 centimetres. You will share this rather palatial residence with anywhere between three and six other birds. This, admittedly, is a little cramped. Being a bird of average size, at rest you need a little over 630 square centimetres to be able to sit down comfortably. If you wanted the luxury of turning around, then you would require just under 1,700 square centimetres. The standard 12 by 20 inch cage, shared with four other chickens, gives you about 300 square centimetres. Total. Just to be clear on the sort of dimensions we're talking about here, 500 square centimetres is about the size of a sheet of A4 paper. If you're a very lucky bird, and share your cage with only three others, then you have 375 square centimetres. Either way, you can forget about stretching your 30 inch (75 cm) wingspan.

Stretching and turning around are not the only things stymied by your close confinement. Any possibility of normal social interaction has also pretty much gone. Chickens have evolved as social creatures, and essential to the stability of any group chickens form is a social hierarchy, known colloquially as the 'pecking order'. In more normal conditions, chickens lower down the order stay out of the way of their more dominant conspecifics. But it's a little difficult to stay out of the way of anything in a 12 by 20 inch cage. So lots of chickens are going to get pecked, and the chances are you are going to be one of them. Indeed, if you are at the bottom of the caged mini-hierarchy, then you may well be pecked to death.

Now, of course, the reason for your debeakings becomes clear. If too many chickens get pecked to death, profits drop. This is a pattern that is repeated time and time again in animal husbandry. An animal is raised in unpleasant and unnatural conditions, and this causes it to behave in unpleasant and unnatural ways. But do we change the conditions? No, that would be unprofitable. Instead, we butcher the animal so that the damage caused by its unpleasant and unnatural behaviour does not eat into our profits too much.

After a few months of constant rubbing against the cage, and other birds pecking at you, you will have lost many, maybe most, of your feathers. Your skin will be red and raw, especially around your tail. You will be suffering from a severe form of osteoporosis, so much so that even being handled by a human may result in the snapping of your legs or wings, and the caving in of your ribcage. By now, you and your cage-mates are demonstrably hysterical, almost certainly insane, and are very probably developing a penchant for cannibalism. After a year or two of this (if you are still alive – 35 per cent of your cage-mates will not be), your productivity will wane, making it unprofitable for the factory owner to feed or house you any longer. You will be delivered to the processors to be turned into stock cubes, frozen pies, or pet food. Such is the life of a battery hen.

If you are born a 'broiler' rather than a layer, then you are a little more fortunate: you won't live as long. A day-old chick, you will, along with anything from 10,000 to several 100,000 other chicks, be sent to a broiler house where you receive the mandatory debeaking. The broiler house is a large, windowless shed. If you are lucky, you will be allowed to live on the floor of this shed, although some producers use tiers of cages to get more birds into the same size shed. At first, you may have some room in which to move around; you and your shed-mates are still small. As you all grow, however, conditions become progressively more cramped. By the time you reach slaughtering weight, after about seven weeks, you may have as little as half a square foot of space.

As you all grow, of course, what grows with you is the mountain of excrement that covers the floor and the acrid stench of ammonia that fills the air. The ammonia is itself a serious health problem. You will, in all likelihood, be suffering from hock burn and breast blisters. How bad can things get? You are being burned by your own (and others') urine. Also littering the floor in gradually increasing numbers are the bodies of your shed-mates. Naturally enough, you are made unhappy by these unnatural conditions and develop various 'vices'. Unable to establish a natural social hierarchy in a flock of 50,000 or more, you have a tendency to fight with your shed-mates and, like your laying sister, a rapidly developing proclivity for cannibalism. But cannibalism, if you will forgive the pun, eats directly into the profits of the owner. So what does he or she do? Ameliorate the conditions that cause your behaviour? Allow you to live in more natural conditions? Give you more room? No, that would reduce profits. Instead, you are debeaked, and the light around you artificially controlled. In many systems, this means that the light is reduced to as little as 2 lux (candlelight is approximately 10 lux). Thus, since reduced lighting has been shown to reduce aggression, you are likely to live out your last few weeks in near darkness.

Basically, it's no contest. Faced with a choice between a life like that and having an alien burst out of my chest, I would invest in some plastic tablecloths and go with the alien every time. And notice that I haven't even gone into our worst abuses of the animals we eat – the sort involved in raising veal calves or intensively reared pigs, for example. Nor have I gone into the way these animals die, which is not the painless, antiseptic death most people imagine.

MIRROR, MIRROR

We do this sort of thing to billions of animals every year. What can justify this appalling treatment? We're pretty sure they're conscious, and suffer these grotesque excesses inflicted on them. So the capacity for consciousness cannot be a relevant difference between us and them – for we both have it. They are, of course, not human, but that can't be a relevant difference here any more than the fact that we were not of the same species as the aliens of *Independence Day* was a relevant difference then. Chickens and pigs are, typically, less intelligent than us – but to regard this as a relevant difference would run bang into the problem of marginal cases. Humans with moderate to severe brain damage, human infants, humans with degenerative brain disorders and so on need be no more intelligent than the average pig – which, despite a bad press, is, in fact, an intelligent and sensitive creature. So, would we treat these humans in the way we now treat pigs? Not unless we were total psychos. They can't use language, and so cannot tell us of their suffering. But this is no more relevant than our inability to communicate telepathically in the *Independence Day* scenario, and the same is true of many humans too.

The horrors that the aliens inflict upon us pale in comparison with the horrors we inflict on billions of animals every year. And, even overlooking our greater barbarity, the aliens have a much better excuse for their treatment of us. When the aliens lay their eggs in us, this is in aid of a vital interest of theirs: reproduction. Reproduction, continuation of yourself and your species is, unarguably, a vital interest of any living thing. Why, on the other hand, do we eat chickens and pigs? Is this a similarly vital interest of ours? Do we need to eat meat in order to survive? Or to be healthy? Of course not, as the existence of millions of healthy vegetarians all over the world attests. We eat meat for one reason and one reason only: we like the taste. When the aliens lay their eggs in us, they condemn us to death, and so rob us of our most vital interest. But at least they do this because of a vital interest of their own. When we treat pigs, chickens, cattle and other animals in the way we do, we inflict lives of untold horror on them and then condemn them to a brutal death – thus also robbing them of their most vital interests. But there is no similarly vital interest of ours at stake.

In the way we treat animals, we fall far short of the core ideals of consistency and impartiality that define our own moral tradition. Are the aliens any worse than us? Are they any more vicious? The reality is, I think, the other way round. If we think of the aliens as warped and evil creatures, maybe we should take a look in the mirror. This, I think, is one of the great merits of science fiction. Many sci-fi themes deal with an encounter with a life form that is inherently alien or *other* to us – and it is difficult to imagine anything more alien or *other* to us than the eponymous villains who made Ripley's life (or rather lives) such a misery. But the encounter with the *other* is always, at the same time, a way of understanding ourselves more closely and clearly. The encounter with otherness acts as a mirror that throws into sharper relief our own emotional, psychological and moral contours.

We can, in fact, put this point in terms of the ideas of the views from the inside and outside. In assessing our own moral status or value, we tend to be blinded by the view from the inside. Being at the centre of this view, we tend to exaggerate our moral importance and merit. We forget that, as moral beings, we also have a view from the outside – a way we look to other creatures. An encounter with something that is irredeemably alien to us is often the best way of both getting us to remember that this view from the outside exists and, to some extent, working out the principal contours revealed by it. As moral creatures, we have to consider not only the way our actions seem from the inside, but also the way they seem from the outside – to the others whose lives they affect.

And this, ultimately, is what the golden rule is all about.

8) STAR WARS
GOOD AND EVIL

GEORGE LUCAS:
TINSELTOWN'S MANICHAEAN

What can you say about George Lucas? As a sci-fi director, he's done it all. As a *sci-phi* director, on the other hand, he's probably not the most subtle of souls. I mean, it's pretty much all black and white for George Lucas – even the side of the Force to which he takes exception is called the *dark* side. But, he did have the unparalleled vision to put Carrie Fisher in a bikini and chain her to Jabba the Hut, and that would merit inclusion in this book on its own. Oh, and that there's the fact that the *Star Wars* trilogy – actually it's not a trilogy any more is it? – is the most successful sci-fi film series ever made. That too.

In these commercially unrivalled series of films, Lucas presents us with a worldview that's usually known as *manichaeanism*, after its Persian founder Mani 'the apostle of God' (*c.* AD 216– 276). According to manichaeans, the world, and especially human life, consists of a colossal struggle between good and evil, which they think is equivalent to both light and dark on the one hand, and God and matter on the other. Good and evil, according to manichaeans, should be understood as equally real and independent principles or features of reality. Which principle is going to win out, nobody knows, but the struggle will go on until one side does. Traditionally, manichaeans have understood themselves as taking the side of light over dark.

It is this sort of manichaeanism that underlies most of what goes on in the *Star Wars* series. The films are concerned with good and evil, light and dark, specifically with the good and evil that is in each one of us, and they deal with the, often complex, relations between these two opposed forces. In each one of us, there is probably a little of both. Can we neatly separate off the one from the other? Can the light in us exist separately from the dark? Is the dark necessarily a bad thing? Or simply misunderstood? These are the sorts of themes that the *Star Wars* sexology attempts to answer.[1]

Star Wars

We'll start, as does George Lucas, with episodes IV–VI, that constitute the original Star Wars trilogy, incorporating the films *Star Wars* (1977), *The Empire Strikes Back* (1980) and *The Return of the Jedi* (1983). This trilogy deals with the relationship between Luke Skywalker (Mark Hamill) and the evil Darth Vader (James Earl Jones' disembodied voice coupled with Dave Prowse's disenvocalled[2] body), who, inevitably, turns out to be Luke's father.

---

1. OK, so I just made 'sexology' up. Actually it's a quintology that's soon to be a sexology. Who knows, by the time this book comes out, it may actually be a sexology.
2. Sorry, did it again.

And this is all set against the backdrop of galactic domination by the evil Empire, run by the equally evil Emperor, whose right-hand man is the evil Lord Vader. So anyway …

A long time ago in a galaxy far, far away … … blah, blah, blah …. What the hell, everyone knows this one anyway. Basically, Luke Skywalker, together with Han Solo (Harrison Ford) and Princess Leia (Carrie Fisher) and a big furry guy called Chewbacca, battle the evil Empire. To cut a long story short – they win. End of story.

If there's anyone out there who hasn't seen the damned films – and yeah, like that's a real possibility – here's a little more detail. Most of you can skip to the next section. Anyway, Luke Skywalker is in fact Darth Vader's son. He's the fruit of the marriage of the evil Lord Vader to Princess Amydala (Natalie Portman) – although we don't find this out until the second series of films, which is essentially a prequel to the first. Of course, the beautiful Ms Portman would not normally copulate with evil tyrants with metal bodies and serious breathing difficulties. But when she copulated with Darth Vader, he wasn't, in fact, Darth Vader at all, but Annakin Skywalker, the Jedi apprentice who would later turn into Darth Vader.

Anyway, Luke was not the only fruit of the loins of Darth and Amydala. In fact, he has a twin sister, and since the only other woman, apart from Amydala, in the movie, or entire series of movies, is Carrie Fisher, she's it by default. When the ghost of Alec Guinness (who plays the – retired – Jedi knight Obi Wan Kenobi) reveals this to Luke, it no doubt comes as bit of a shock, since he's clearly been thinking about shagging her for the past two films. But there you are. Anyway, some time after impreg-nating Natalie Portman with Luke and Leia, Darth Vader turns to the *dark side* of the Force, and comes under the thrall of the evil Emperor. It's then that he becomes Darth Vader, having until then been Annakin Skywalker.

So, off he goes to build an empire, while Luke gets sent off to live in a desert craphole and Leia becomes some sort of princess and senator. However, they both become involved in the rebellion against the Empire, and their paths fortuitously become intertwined. Luke and Leia, together with a young Harrison Ford, manage to deal the Empire a series of embarrassing defeats, including the notable destruction of the Death Star in the first film. This is helped by the fact that the Force is strong in Luke, and he has trained as a Jedi knight, the ancient order of guardians of the galaxy whose power was based on a mystical attunement to the mysterious Force that supposedly permeates and animates the entire universe. The series culminates in *The Return of the Jedi*, where Darth Vader redeems himself by destroying the Emperor just as the Emperor is about to kill Luke, and dies in the process. So, in death, Darth Vader returns to the light side, or, at least, non-dark side, of the Force.

The second series of films began with *The Phantom Menace* (2000) and continued with the improbably entitled *Attack of the Clones* (2002). At the time of writing, the third and final instal-ment has not been released.[3] This series is a prequel to the first, and deals with Annakin Skywalker's seduction by the dark side of the Force, and his transition from the sweet little blond-haired

---

3. Known as Episode III, it is due for release in 2005.

kid (actually, I thought he was an annoying little shit – but let's not get into that) into the evil Darth Vader. Or I'm assuming it does, because that's in the next film that's not out yet (at the end of the second movie, all we really have by way of evidence is that he has one of Darth's trademark artificial bodily appendages – circumstantial, but it's not really going to stand up in court). After impressing in a hovercraft race that owed a lot to the chariot race in the 1950s film *Ben Hur*, Annakin is taken on as a Jedi apprentice by a young Obi Wan Kenobi – played by Ewan MacGregor doing his best to sound like Alec Guinness. When he gets older, Annakin (now played by Hayden Christiansson) falls in love with Natalie Portman, playing Princess Amydala. And, after foiling a plot against the Republic (again), Annakin leaves the Jedi order, marries Amydala, impregnates her with Luke and Leia, and promptly turns to the dark side.

Two things always struck me as strange about this, worries that I have never had satisfactorily answered. First of all, why is it that in six films we find essentially only two women – both of whom are ex-princesses sidelining as senators? Couldn't they have been just a little different? Just a smidgin? When he wrote *The Phantom Menace*, and needed some background for his only major female character of Episodes I–III, did he just turn to episodes IV–VI, find the only major female character of that trilogy, and press the 'copy and paste' functions on his computer? Secondly, 'Luke Skywalker', great name. Cool. 'Darth Vader', ditto. But 'Han Solo'? A little *Man From Uncle*-ish, don't you think. And by the time you get to Princess Amydala, George has apparently lost interest to such an extent that he's looking to human body parts as the inspiration for his characters' names. I'm confidently expecting a Princess Vulva to make her appearance in the final instalment.

PLATO: EVIL AS THE ABSENCE OF GOOD

According to *Star Wars*, evil exists. It is real. And it is everywhere. It exists as the dark side to a force – sorry, *the* Force – that permeates and animates the whole of the universe and everything in it. In earlier – more *Inquisitional* – times, George could have expected to be burned at the stake for endorsing this view.[4] Indeed, manichaeanism was, at one time – inaccurately – regarded as simply an heretical sect of Christianity, rather than a separate religion.[5] So, in endorsing this essentially manichaean position, George is pretty much swimming against the official doctrine of the Christian Church that has always regarded evil not as something that is real but simply an absence or lack of something real – the absence of good.

The Christian Church, of course, didn't get this idea from nowhere. Still less was it an original idea of theirs. Heaven forbid. The idea that evil is not a real, independent feature of the world but simply an absence of good has a long and distinguished philosophical history, stretching all the way back to the ancient Greek philosopher Plato (*c.* 428–348 BC), and possibly further. According to Plato, ultimate reality consists in a sort of pure and perfect goodness. To the extent anything diverges from this, it

---

4. I say 'expected' but, on the other hand, *nobody* expects the Spanish Inquisition.
5. Consensus now favours the view that it is a separate religion.

not only becomes less good, it becomes less real too. And the ultimate goal of human life is to attain true knowledge of what he called the *form of the good*.

Plato's idea of a *form* has seeped into modern usage. We say, for example, that someone is (or isn't) in good form. The athlete on a current run of success in his or her sport is said to be in good form. So too is the person who comes into work happy and cheerful, as opposed to the miserable sod they usually are. The word 'form', here, goes all the way back to Plato. If we knew our philology – our linguistic history – then we would know that what we are saying, when we say that someone is in good form, is that they are pretty close to being a perfect example of their kind. And this all stems from Plato's metaphysics – his account of the ultimate nature of reality.

Plato had something like this in mind. Some things are better examples of their kinds than other things. Plato – a self-confessed mathematics geek – had some idea that mathematics mirrored the true structure of reality, or something like that,[6] so let's use the sort of example he would have liked. Suppose we have some circles drawn on paper. Some of them will be better renditions of circles than others. Some will be more like ovals than circles, for example. But we can clearly distinguish which circles provide the best examples of circles and which provide the worst. How are we able to do this?

In one way or another, we must have some sort of basis for

---

6. An idea he got from the Pythagoreans, founded by Pythagoras (c. 572–510 BC). We all know him from the square of the hypotenuse is equal to the sum of the squares on the other two sides of a triangle idea.

comparison. If we can distinguish good from bad examples of circles, and all grades of good and bad in between, then we must have some idea of what a perfect circle would be like. If we had no such idea, how could we separate off the good from the bad, the superior from the inferior examples of circles? So let's assume that we must have some idea of what a perfect circle would be like, and it is this idea that allows us to distinguish good from bad versions of circles. From where do we get this idea?

Plato's answer is that we cannot have got it from anywhere in the physical world. No matter how careful we are in drawing circles, and no matter what the precision of the instruments we use to draw them, there will always be some flaw in our drawing. There will always be some deviation from perfection in the circle we have drawn. And this is true of all physical circles. No matter how skilfully drawn, they will always deviate in at least some small way from perfect circularity. But if we can't have acquired the idea from the physical world, from where can we have got it?

According to Plato, we got it from somewhere *outside* the physical world. There must, he concludes, be some other world, some non-physical realm of being, and in this realm reside things like perfect circles. Not just perfect circles, perfect everythings. In this non-physical realm of being there exists a perfect man, a perfect woman, a perfect horse, a perfect triangle, a perfect cloud, a perfect sword (or light sabre) and so on. These perfect exemplars of things, Plato referred to as *forms*, and this non-physical realm that contained them, he called the *world of forms*.

These forms were, according to Plato, arranged hierarchically, and at the summit of this hierarchy was what Plato called the *form of the good*, what we might call *goodness itself*. The idea behind this is pretty much the same as in the case of circles. Various people, actions, rules, institutions are, at least in our eyes, good. Some of these things are also bad. And in between there are various gradations of good and bad. But even the things we regard as good are not perfectly good. No matter how good a person is, for example, they could always be better. They will always contain some slight moral imperfection, some deviation, some divergence, no matter how slight, from perfect goodness. And, when this happens, the person who is suitably equipped in the moral sensibility department will be able to discern this departure from perfect goodness.

This, for Plato, indicates that we have the idea, however vague and inchoate, of perfect goodness – at least if we are suitably morally trained. We can't have acquired this idea from the physical world, for nothing in that world is perfectly good. Therefore, there must be some other world – a non-physical realm of being – where this perfect goodness, the *form of the good*, exists. And this world is, of course, the non-physical world of forms.

So, in addition to the ordinary physical world, Plato asserted the existence of a non-physical world of forms. However, according to Plato, not only does this non-physical world of forms exist, it is, in fact, more real than the ordinary physical world. He had two reasons for this. The first was based on his preference for the eternal and unchanging over the shifting and ephemeral. The ordinary physical world is constantly changing, things coming into existence and going out of existence, and altering in countless ways through time. But the real – that is, the *really* real – for

Plato, must be eternal and unchanging. This can't be the ordinary physical world; therefore it must be the world of forms. So it is the world of forms that is (really) real, and reality of the physical world, to the extent that it is real at all, derives from the world of forms. Secondly, any individual thing – say a circle drawn on paper – is what it is only because of its relation to a form. What makes the thing drawn on paper a circle is that it somehow resembles the form of circularity, perfect circularity. So, Plato concludes, what makes any physical thing the thing it is, is its relation to a form. But the same is not true of forms. Any form is the form that it is completely independently of its relation to physical things. And this, Plato concludes, shows that the forms are more real than physical things.

Plato used a famous analogy to explain the derivative and secondary status of the physical world: the analogy of the cave. Imagine you are prisoner in a cave. There you sit, chained to a post with a group of other prisoners. Worse still, you have lived your entire life as a prisoner in this cave. The only source of light in the cave is a fire, and this casts shadows on the wall behind you. Because of your predicament, you mistake these shadows for reality. You know no better; your life has been one of shadows. This is the situation of the average person – a prisoner in the physical world mistaking shadows of reality for reality.

One day, however, you escape from your chains and make your way to the mouth of the cave. At first, the light is too harsh, and you have to content yourself by looking at the shadows on the cave wall – this time cast by the sun, not the fire. Eventually, after suitable preparation, you are able to venture into the outside world and see not shadows but the real objects that are their source. One day, you may even be able to look directly at the sun. Escaping from the cave is analogous to the process of becoming a philosopher. Gradually, step by step, you are able to acquaint yourself with things that are more and more real. The visible objects you are eventually able to look at correspond to the forms, and the source of their visibility – the sun – corresponds to the form of the good.

So, according to Plato, ordinary physical things and the ordinary physical world derive whatever reality they have from the world of forms – as shadows derive whatever reality they have from that which casts them. And so the physical world, for Plato, is real only to the extent that it relates to the world of forms. The reality of the world of forms is primary. The reality of physical things depends on the extent to which they resemble the relevant forms. And in so far as they deviate from their relevant form, they not only become less perfect, they become less real.

However, as we have seen, the most important of the forms, and hence the most real, is, for Plato, the form of the good. So, according to Plato, in so far as things deviate from the form of the good, they become less real. There is no form of the bad, no form of evil, at least not according to Plato. Evil is simply an absence, a hiatus, a lack: it is the absence of good. And what this means, for all intents and purposes, is that evil is unreal. Evil is an illusion. The more evil something becomes, the less real it also, thereby, becomes.

So, if Plato is right, when Annakin Skywalker converted to the dark side, and became Darth Vader, he not only became less perfect, he also became less real. This, of course, flies in the face of George Lucas's position in *Star Wars*. Darth Vader, despite being hidden behind a cloak, mask and helmet for the three films, is the most real character in them. His presence, and his evil, is palpable. He is not simply an absence or hiatus in the films. He is, in effect, the whole point of the story. And, similarly, for his evil acts. When, in conjunction with Peter Cushing as the admiral, he uses the Death Star to destroy a planet early on, this evil action is not simply an absence or tear in the fabric of reality. On the contrary, it partly constitutes that fabric.

I think we have to go with George Lucas over Plato and the Christian Church. Evil exists, and not simply as an illusion or absence of what is good. The evil actions performed by Lord Vader are evil for what they are in themselves, and not simply because they are lacking in something else.

RIPPING OFF PLATO

Darth Vader, of course, is not the sort of person you can imagine going to heaven. If they're going to allow people who tyrannise entire galaxies and destroy entire planets merely on a whim into heaven, then they're basically going to let anyone in: lawyers, estate agents, the whole shebang. And there goes the neighbourhood. So Christian metaphysics has no place for Darth Vader in the greater scheme of things. He's going downstairs if anyone is.

And this is not surprising really – because Christian metaphysics is deeply indebted to Plato, in the way you are deeply indebted to someone whose ideas you've just stolen. What we get with Plato, for the first time really, is a genuine philosophical defence of the notion of a non-physical reality – not only that, but a non-physical reality that is more real than the physical one. This idea was appropriated by the Roman neoplatonist Plotinus (*c.* 204–270 AD), and then worked its way down to a guy called Augustine – *St* Augustine of Hippo (354–430 AD) that is. And Augustine incorporated the idea of a non-physical reality into Christian metaphysics. Before this time, Christianity didn't really have any time for anything non-physical. It was all resurrection of the (physical) body on Judgment Day, rather than the survival of a non-physical soul in heaven. Augustine changed all that. Now we get the soul as a non-physical thing, modelled on Plato's world of forms, which, in turn, becomes transmogrified into heaven. You get the picture.

So, heaven becomes the truly real. The Earth – and our earthly bodies – what are they good for? Well, basically, getting us into heaven. The justification for our existence here is for us to get to heaven – to live whatever lives and to pass whatever tests are necessary for us to go upstairs, rather than downstairs. Also, we get a characteristic attitude towards evil. Since the justification for our existence lies in heaven, and since there can be no place for evil in heaven, what we have to do is excise from ourselves whatever elements of evil we find there. The evil parts of us we have to stamp out, extirpate, eradicate. And so we get the characteristic Christian attitude towards the evil, or at least questionable, parts of us. If thy hand offend thee, cut it off. If thy eye offend thee, pluck it out, and all that medieval stuff. The dark side of our character is something to be, basically, given a good kicking.

DIONYSUS VERSUS the CRUCIFIED

Friedrich Nietzsche (1844–1900) was one philosopher who wouldn't have any of this. Indeed, towards the end of his life, Nietzsche explicitly, or as explicitly as he ever got, defined his position in opposition to Christianity: 'Have I been understood? – *Dionysus against the Crucified.*' Of course, Nietzsche was largely insane by the time he wrote this – almost certainly the result of a syphilitic infection picked up during a youthful indiscretion at a whorehouse. Since this was Nietzsche's only youthful indiscretion at a whorehouse, and arguably his only youthful indiscretion of any kind, you have to feel that he was a little unlucky on this one.

What does he mean, 'Dionysus against the Crucified'? First of all, take Dionysus. In his first book, *The Birth of Tragedy*, Nietzsche argued for a certain view of the ancient Greek psyche. The genius of the Greeks – with their art, their architecture, their philosophy and so on – lay in what Nietzsche was later to call *sublimation*. The Greeks were basically a very *dark* bunch of people. All sorts of dark desires, feelings, drives were present in the Greek mentality, simmering away just below the surface. Occasionally they gave in to these impulses, and engaged in festivals dedicated to Dionysus, the god of the vine. These went on for days or even weeks, and involved a lot of drinking, general debauchery, and lots and lots of sex. The echoes of these festivals can, of course, be found today in Ibiza, Corfu and places like that. But today's version is tame compared to the Greeks. They *really* knew how to party. Alternatively, as Darth would put it, they appreciated the power of the dark side.

But what was noticeable for Nietzsche is that when they weren't being totally degenerate the Greeks were actually good at a lot of things. In art, architecture, philosophy and so on, they produced a culture that was arguably the greatest the world has ever seen. How, one might think, did they manage to do this when, beneath a thin veneer, they were a bunch of debauched, perverted, debased and corrupted lager louts? Nietzsche's answer was that they did not produce the greatest culture the world has even seen *despite* being a bunch of sicko miscreants, but *because* of it. The dark side lurking in the Greeks was not an *impediment* to their greatness, it was an *impetus* to it. And the key to under-standing Nietzsche's view lies in the concept of *sublimation*.

Suppose the dark side of the Force is strong in you. So you have various dark urges and desires, ones perhaps that you don't fully recognise or understand. But these desires are there, and domination of the entire galaxy is high up on the list of them. What should you do about this dark side of your character? Well, it seems, you have three options.

The first is what Nietzsche regarded as the *Christian* option. Deny these desires. Extirpate them; stamp them out. These are bad desires, evil ones, they must be repudiated, renounced, rejected. So, if you take the Christian option, then instead of destroying a few planets before breakfast, you will stay at home and fret about your sinful state. You will very much regret your corrupt and wicked character, and do everything in your power to emasculate it. This will involve something like cutting off and plucking out, metaphorically speaking, your various parts that have gone and offended you.

It is, of course, difficult to imagine Lord Vader sitting at home fretting about his character shortcomings. Besides, a metaphorical strategy that involved plucking out and cutting off offensive parts of you could be easily misconstrued – how easily we tend to run together the literal and metaphorical – and this would be disastrous for Darth: he's running seriously short on body parts anyway.

More seriously, the Christian strategy has, according to Nietzsche, had two drawbacks. First of all, a vital opportunity for self-improvement has been lost. These primitive drives – drives to destroy, conquer, dominate – are the source of a substantial amount of energy, and all the energy – the power – with which they would provide you has been lost in the attempt to renounce them. Secondly, this attempt at repudiation and rejection is both futile and unhealthy. Drives – and the power they contain – can never be destroyed or renounced, merely converted into another form. And if they are not given outward expression, they will find an alternative form of inward expression. In particular, the failure to give expression to a powerful drive results in that drive being turned back against the person who has it. The typical result of this is illness – psychological, physical or both. Today, we refer to this general idea as *repression*, an idea made famous by Freud, and then popularised by a succession of imitators. For example, Freud's account of hysterical illness involved the idea that a powerful drive or feelings of which the subject is ashamed – and Freud, of course, emphasised the sexual drives – is repressed by the subject and so comes to manifest itself in another way – say as *hysterical paralysis*; the subject becomes paralysed even though there is nothing physically wrong with her. The connected ideas of repression and psychosomatic disorder, and the by now hackneyed advice not to bottle things up inside, all have their roots in Nietzsche.

So, Lord Vader is to be congratulated for at least one thing: not bottling up his drives and feelings. Evil bastard he may be, but he is certainly not a repressed or neurotic one. But what are we to do to if the galactic domination thing is not really our bag but, at the same time, we don't want to become neurotic? If we cannot utilise the Christian strategy of denying or renouncing our drives, what are the alternatives? Well, the obvious one is to let it all hang out, baby. If you want to destroy a few planets, crush a few rebel uprisings, and place the galaxy under the thrall of an evil despot, then *go for it*! Who is anyone else to judge you? Bottling these feelings up inside is a surefire way of ending up repressed and unhealthy. So – express yourself, dude. Nietzsche didn't give this strategy a name. We might call it the *hippy* strategy, not, of course, because hippies are abnormally interested in galactic domination, but because of the general idea of letting everything hang out.

Nietzsche would hate this strategy too. Admittedly, adopting it might allow you to avoid many of the adverse psychological and physical consequences of the Christian strategy. But it too has its drawbacks. Most importantly, a golden opportunity for self-improvement has been lost. All the energy and power provided by the drives for domination, destruction and conquest has been lost. The energy has gone precisely into dominating, destroying and conquering the galaxy. Fun, undoubtedly, but hardly edifying. At least, not in Nietzsche's view. While the Christian strategy of repression leaves you worse off than you were, the hippy strategy leaves you no better than you were before.

Greatness, in Nietzsche's view, is going to be achieved neither by repression nor free expression of your most powerful desires and drives. Rather, it requires something quite different: *sublimation*. The basic idea is that powerful drives and desires can be transformed into something else – into quite different and, in Nietzsche's view at least, more worthwhile drives and desires. Their ultimate outward expression, therefore, can be very different from the drive or desire that provides its underlying force or power.

The various dark drives and desires possessed by Darth are, according to Nietzsche, susceptible to an indefinite number of transformations. The key to greatness is the ability to transform these desires according to your *will*. In the original *Star Wars* trilogy, Darth is simply swept along by his drives, a prisoner of them rather than their master. Greatness, for Darth and for all the rest of us too, is to become master of our drives without – and this is the crux – *weakening* them. Instead of trying to stamp out the drives, and instead of simply giving them free rein, you transform them into some other – and more worthwhile – drive. So Darth should take his desire to, for example, crush a rebel uprising by destroying their planet, and sublimate this desire, transform or channel it into something else – maybe stay in and write that novel, paint that picture or compose that symphony. The force of the original drive is redirected into this new activity, and if this sublimation is done properly, Darth has the chance of becoming a genius in one of his newly adopted fields. For genius, according to Nietzsche, is simply sublimated power. So, far from being an impediment to his writing, painting, or composing, Darth's dark desires for planetary destruction are necessary conditions of it.

The capacity for greatness, in Nietzsche's view, is essentially bound up with the ability to sublimate – transform, redirect or channel – your primitive drives and desires into higher ones: more artistic and, ultimately, more spiritual drives. We might call this the *Nietzschean* strategy. A war on your primitive drives and desires will leave you depleted, and in all likelihood diseased. Free expression of your drives will leave you, above all, *average*. The possibility of greatness requires sublimation, rather than repression or expression, of your primitive drives and desires.

The stronger these primitive drives and desires are, the more you have the potential in you for greatness if – and this is the trick – you are able to sublimate them appropriately. The strength of a person's basic and primitive drives will, according to Nietzsche, vary from person to person. And their strength is a measure of the health of a person: the stronger the basic drives, the healthier, in principle, is the person who has them. The person with strong basic drives, who has attained the ability to sublimate these drives continually into higher and higher forms, is what Nietzsche refers to as an *ubermensch*: an *overman* or *superman*. An *overman* is, basically, a highly sublimated bastard.

Most of us, hopefully, don't have any serious desires for planetary destruction, domination or conquest. Maybe most of the desires we are ashamed of tend to be of the nakedly hedonistic rather than violent or destructive kind. But the same point applies. Instead of dropping a few Es and heading off to visit the latest object of your sexual fixation, you can take these drives and sublimate them – transform them into something entirely more noble. In this process – a continual process of sublimation and resublimation, Nietzsche thought – lies the only real possibility of greatness.

Indeed, for Nietzsche, the same sort of point applies not only to individuals, but also to cultures. It is the fact that the Greeks, as a culture, were so *dark* – that they appreciated the power of the dark side – that is the ultimate source of their greatness. 'The greater and the more terrible the passions that an age, a people, an individual can permit themselves, because they are capable of employing them as a means, the higher stands their culture.'[7]

LIVE YOUR LIFE AS A WORK OF ART

In Nietzsche's epigram, 'Dionysus versus the Crucified', Dionysus represents the *overman*, the person with powerful basic drives who continually sublimates these drives into increasingly higher and higher forms. The contrast with 'the Crucified' could not be more stark. The Crucified represents the person who wastes his or her life in a futile and self-destructive attempt to renounce and reject these drives.

Where does our friend Darth fit into this scheme? Well, I think we can safely say he's not the sort to sit at home in a futile and self-destructive attempt to renounce his primitive desires. What we called the Christian strategy is not the great Lord Vader's bag at all, baby. Does this mean he is a Nietzschean *ubermensch*?

---

7. Nietzsche, *The Twilight of the Gods.*

Not quite. Nietzsche's view would, I think, be that Darth is a tragically flawed attempt at an *overman*. The potential was there, but he didn't quite cut it. Let's see why.

First of all, why bother with all this *overman* stuff? After all, isn't dropping some Es, getting wasted, and pursuing the object of your sexual desires far more fun than sitting at home writing, or painting, or composing God knows what? And surely even destroying a few planets has a certain *je ne sais quoi*, that elevates it above the mundane process of artistic creation? In particular, wouldn't you be much *happier* adopting the hippy strategy rather than the Nietzschean one? Maybe, but so what? Underlying this thought is the tacit assumption that life is all about being happy (the view that, in the previous chapter, we identified as *hedonism*). Nietzsche would reject this assumption absolutely. He hated hedonism, he hated utilitarianism, and, by proxy, the country from which it originated: 'Man does not strive for happiness; only the English do that.'

We are not, according to Nietzsche, here to be happy, at least not if we mean by that the sort of simple pleasure often associated with utilitarianism. If there is a meaning to your life, it is *aesthetic*, rather than hedonistic, in nature: 'Only as an aesthetic phenomenon is life and the existence of man eternally justified.' We should, Nietzsche claims, lives our lives as works of art.

Living your life as a work of art involves – according to the standard Nietzschean recipe – constantly overcoming yourself, continually sublimating your drives and desires and so turning them into higher ones. And, crucially, it involves doing this in a balanced way. Restraint, not licence, is the key to the aesthetically pleasing life. Darth Vader falls short of Nietzsche's requirements. While it is true that Darth has clearly tapped in to his dark side, it is also true that he has failed to achieve the required level of sublimation necessary to becoming an *overman*. The drives to dominate, control and destroy are all fairly primitive drives. Lord Vader seems far more concerned with simply expressing, acting upon, these primitive drives, rather than trying to sublimate them into something higher. The result is not an *overman* but an unbalanced megalomaniac.

The Force was strong in Annakin Skywalker. Also, strong was his dark side, and this made Darth Vader a man of potential greatness. If your basic drives are not strong enough, if they are in any way weak or attenuated, then you will not even have the capacity to become an *overman*. And the basic drives were admittedly very strong in Annakin Skywalker. However, his transformation to Darth Vader seems to consist largely in letting these dark drives and desires have free rein. And this is why he could never be a Nietzschean *overman*. To do that, sublimation – continual transformation of one's basic drives into progressively higher and higher forms – is necessary. And this is what was lost in the transformation of Annakin Skywalker into Darth Vader.

Nietzsche's attitude towards Darth Vader would probably be something like his attitude towards Cesare Borgia. In his last work, *Ecce Homo* ('Behold the Man'), Nietzsche quips that he would prefer even a Cesare Borgia to a Parsifal (a figure from German mythology who provides the central character for one of Wagner's operas). Parsifal represents the 'Christian' type, the man of weak passions and drives, or the man engaged in stamping out his passions and drives. Cesare Borgia represents the man of unconstrained passions – a man of legendary excess and infamous cruelty. Nietzsche prefers even Borgia to Parsifal. Why? Because at least the *potential* for greatness was there. Cesare Borgia is preferable to Parsifal because, while he falls very far short of greatness, he at least had the potential for greatness – it lay there in the strength and intensity of his basic drives. If only he could have learned to sublimate them, then greatness was his for the taking.

Cesare Borgia aside, Nietzsche's attitude to Darth Vader is, perhaps, best reflected in his attitude towards Napoleon. Nietzsche both admired and despised Napoleon – regarding him as a mixture of *ubermensch* and *unmensch*. As more than human and less than human. His greatness, for Nietzsche, lay not in his military successes, but in the fact that he was able to discipline, to sublimate, his drives and desires to make himself greater than he would otherwise have been. But, in the end, this process of sublimation was partial and incomplete, and we find ourselves left with his many inhuman qualities. Napoleon, according to Nietzsche, 'had been corrupted by the means he *had* to employ, and had *lost* the *nobility* of his character'. The process of sublimation is a continual one, and its reward is only itself. It does not lend itself to short-term expediency of the sort necessary to conquer most of Europe. Thus, Napoleon's sublimation, and transformation into an *overman*, was ultimately cut short by his lust to dominate, and the methods he had to employ in satisfying that lust. And this, I think, is a pretty good assessment of the life of Darth Vader.

In what sense is Darth Vader a bad guy? I mean, what did he do that was so bad anyway? If it's just trying to kill Mark Hamill, then I think none of us would really have a problem with that (fathering him – as it turns out he did – now that's a different story). Is our antipathy to Darth just a product of our implicitly Platonic/Christian value system? Should we instead regard Lord Vader as a sort of Nietzschean superhero, revelling in the creativity that his dark side makes possible? Not really. Darth is a mixture of *ubermensch* and *unmensch*. His life was no work of art. His fear (alluded to towards the end of *The Phantom Menace*) led to his lust to dominate; to fear something leads to the desire to control that thing. And his lust to dominate led to the cutting short of the continuous process of sublimation that might, ultimately, have led him to true greatness. Bummer!

On the other hand, it is difficult to imagine what the *Star Wars* films would have been like if Darth had managed to become an *overman*. If we are to take Nietzsche seriously, we would probably find this big guy in a black cloak and helmet shooting off to different parts of the galaxy because he needed to do some research for his book, or because there was a particularly beautiful waterfall he wanted to paint. It is difficult to see this making George Lucas countless millions. And if this is what being an *overman* is, I think I would opt for being the evil version of Lord Vader any day. Being flawed is, clearly, a lot more fun.

9 BLADE RUNNER
DEATH AND THE MEANING OF LIFE

I WANT MORE LIFE!

No book on *sci-phi* would, of course, be complete without an examination of what many people think is the greatest sci-fi film ever made – Ridley Scott's classic, *Blade Runner* (1982).

Los Angeles in the year 2019. And what a dump it is! The majority of the Earth's population has moved *off-world* – that is, to other planets – with only misfits of various stripes left behind. And who can blame them? In the Los Angeles of 2019 it's always raining. Off-world has other attractions besides climatic ones, however. In particular, most of the crappy jobs that no one wants are done by so called *replicants*. These are biologically engineered humanoid life forms, a combination of robot and organism. They are almost indistinguishable from human beings, but with vastly superior strength, agility, endurance and, indeed, intelligence. Replicants have been created in the laboratories of the Tyrell Corporation, for the purpose of performing dangerous, menial, or simply unpleasant tasks off-world. There are replicant soldiers, replicant police officers, replicant janitors (sorry, sanitary engineers), even replicant hookers.

Following an off-world rebellion of replicants – a sort of 'replicants of the (off-) world unite, you have nothing to lose but your crappy jobs' affair – replicants were banished from Earth – on pain of death. Elite squads – known as *blade runners* – were set up to hunt down and kill rogue replicants who returned to Earth. And killing a replicant – as the introductory blurb at the beginning of the movie informs us – is not called execution, it's called *retirement*.

Infiltrating the derelict and desolate society that Earth has become are four replicants – Roy, Leon, Pris and Zhora. These are Nexus VI replicants, top of the line models, and they are led by Roy, played, in surely the greatest role of his career, by Rutger Hauer.[1] Roy is a soldier replicant, and Pris (Daryl Hannah) is the hooker replicant that provides the love interest, or at least his love interest. They have hijacked a space shuttle somewhere off-world, killed its crew and passengers, and headed to Earth, specifically, Los Angeles. Why? Well, the thing about replicants is that they have been engineered to have a lifespan of no more than four years. Eldon Tyrrell, the genius behind the Tyrell Corporation, explains that this has something to do with the development of emotions. They are designed not to have emotions, but after a certain length of time, they begin to develop emotional responses to things. Not wanting there to be replicants running around with emotions – like hatred of their crappy jobs, and resentment of the people who force them to do the crappy jobs, for example – a fail-safe has been built into them: they die after four years. Roy, Pris, Leon and Zhora are all three years into their four-year

---

1. Zenith of his career as scriptwriter as well as actor. Rutger apparently wrote the 'death soliloquy' himself. Brilliant.

stint, and have come to Earth looking for ways to extend their lives. Or, as Roy memorably puts it when meeting Eldon Tyrell, his maker: 'I want more life, fucker!'

Harrison Ford plays Deckard, a particularly burnt-out example of a blade runner who has, in his eyes, retired, but is blackmailed into doing one last job by his ex-boss. In the course of his investigation, he meets Sean Young, a replicant who doesn't know she's a replicant, and, of course, falls in love with her. This basically opens his eyes to the status of replicants. (This is no bad thing, for as Philip K. Dick's original tale, and the Director's Cut of the film seem to suggest, he himself is one.) They are, or certainly seem to be, emotionally and intellectually sensitive creatures, with a clear sense of their own mortality, and a corresponding fear of death. And mortality is, in a sense (as Barry Norman would put it), what the film is all about. Deckard's growing awareness of the true nature of replicants doesn't stop him whacking most of them – although to be fair, much of this is done in self-defence. I mean, if Daryl Hannah is going to insist on wrapping her thighs around your face, she's just asking to be offed, isn't she? However, Deckard's transformation is completed when he is spared by Roy, who has him at his mercy. Roy then dies, and in perhaps the most moving death soliloquy in cinematic history, leaves us with the following words, ones that nicely capture the human (and also, apparently, the replicant) predicament: 'I've seen things you people wouldn't believe. I've entered attack ships on fire off the shoulder of Orion. I've watched sea-beams dance by the Tannhauser gate. Now all these moments will be lost in time, like tears in rain. Time to die.'

IS DEATH A BAD THING?

In what sense, if any, is death a *bad thing*? Not in general, but for the person who dies? In general, for example, death might be quite a good thing – it counteracts overcrowding, safeguards genetic variation. Or whatever. And the death of individual people – Hitler or Osama bin Laden are obvious examples – might be of great benefit to other people. But, except in thankfully rare cases, death has no benefit for the person who undergoes it. Indeed, death, it is usually assumed, *harms* that person. Roy and his gang of replicants certainly assume this, and most of us share that assumption.

We needn't assume this, of course. Death harms the person who dies only if death is, genuinely, the *end*: the cessation of that person. And perhaps it is not. Perhaps we do all go to heaven, and live out eternity in a state of bliss. Or perhaps some of us do. But I'm going to assume that death is the end. If you are one of those lucky people who can bring themselves to not believe this, then you should merely reformulate the question: in what sense is the end of oneself – whenever that occurs – a bad thing? Is death, or the end of oneself, a bad thing? Or, if you think it never occurs, then ask yourself *if* it occurred then *would* it be a bad thing, and, if so, why?

In this culture, of course, we are conditioned to think of this sort of question as unhealthily morbid. Why don't I just lighten up? But, in fact, I'm not going to be talking about death just for the sake of it. I'm really far more interested in why life is a good thing rather than why death is a bad thing. Roy and his replicants wanted to avoid death because they wanted more life. And the underlying assumption here is that life is a good thing – another assumption that we, typically, share with Roy. Death is what takes away life. So, if we can work out why death is a bad thing, then this may tell us why life is a good thing. That is, if we can work out the value of what death takes away, then we can, so the idea goes, work out the value of life. And if we can work out the *value* of life, then, who knows, maybe, just maybe, we can make some headway on the question with which this book opened: the *meaning* of life.

the epicurean argument

Working out why death is a bad thing is not as easy as you might think. The problem stems from the fact that death, whatever else it is, is not something that occurs *in* a life. Death, as the philosopher Ludwig Wittgenstein put it, is the *limit* of a life, and a limit of a life is not something that can occur within that life, any more than the limit of a visual field is something that can occur within that field. A limit of some thing is not part of that thing – otherwise it wouldn't be the limit of it.

If we accept this, then we are immediately faced with a well-known argument, associated with the ancient Greek philosopher Epicurus, an argument that death cannot be something that harms us. It goes like this. Death cannot harm us because while we are alive death has not yet happened (and so can't have harmed us yet), and after we are dead there is nothing left to harm. Death can't harm us until it actually happens, but when it happens we are no longer around for it to harm. But if death cannot harm us, then death is not a bad thing, at least not for the person who dies.

What's wrong with this argument? Indeed, is there anything wrong with it?

Death and Deprivation

If death is the limit of a life, then it does not occur in that life. That seems undeniable. The only way death could harm us is if there exist some types of harm that are not strictly tied to the time at which the event that brings them about occurs. So, for example, even if someone's death occurs at time t, the harm that this death brings with it is not restricted to that time. This, it seems, is the only way that death could harm us, because we are not around when the event of death occurs. So, the question is: are there harms of this sort?

I think there are. There are certain types of harm that are, as we might say, *temporally extended*. What this means, roughly, is that they are harms that cannot, by definition, exist *at* any particular time, but only *through* time – in the relation between one time and a later time. A classic example of this type of harm is what philosophers refer to as *harms of deprivation*.

For example, suppose Eldon Tyrell is attacked by Roy, as in the movie. Roy starts squeezing his head and so on. But suppose Roy is having a bad day at the office, gets a bit sloppy, and does not finish the job. So Tyrell is left not dead but with severe brain trauma, an injury so severe as to reduce him (permanently) to a mental age of, say, three months. Tyrell is, most of us would accept, harmed by the injury and resulting brain damage. But how exactly is it that he is harmed? Before the injury occurred, he could have been happy enough. But so too can he be equally happy after the injury – it's just that he is now happy in a very different way. Before the injury, it was playing chess and designing replicants that made him happy. After the injury, happiness is a clean, dry nappy. Most of us would accept that Tyrell is harmed by the brain damage. But the harm shows itself neither in his condition before the injury, nor in his condition after the injury, but only in the *relation*, and especially the *contrast*, between how he was before and how he was after. The harm that he suffers consists in being deprived of his former condition, and this deprivation exists only in the relation between his condition before the injury and his condition after.

So, harms of deprivation are ones that exist not *at* any particular time, but only *through* time. If we are to understand how death can harm us, the first step is to see that death is a harm of deprivation. Death harms us because of what it takes away. And, as such, the harm of death is a harm that exists through time rather than at any particular time.

The analogy of death with brain injury is, of course, not perfect. In the case of the brain injury, there exists a person both before and after the injury, it's just that it is not clear whether it is the *same* person. But in the case of death, there is no person at all after the death has occurred. This, however, does not really count against the analogy. For, as we saw in Chapter 4, what a person is can best be accounted for in terms of the notion of psychological continuity. And, if this is right, the person – Tyrell – who was around before the brain damage occurred is almost certainly not the same person as the one who is around after the brain damage occurred. There is no sort of psychological continuity between the former person and the latter. So psychologically discontinuous are the two people, not only is the later one a different person from the earlier one, the later one is not even a survivor of the earlier one. The person, Eldon Tyrell, who was around before the brain injury has genuinely ceased to exist when that damage occurs. The brain damage is a limit to his existence just as we are imagining death to be a limit to a life. So, when the damage occurs, Tyrell is no longer around to be harmed. Nevertheless, Tyrell is harmed. What we need to understand is: how is this possible? What is the nature of the harm such that a person can be harmed by death (or severe brain damage) even if they are no longer around to be harmed? To say that death is a harm of deprivation – that it harms us because it deprives us of something – is only a first step. What we now need to understand is something even more basic: how can a deprivation harm us if we are no longer around when the deprivation occurs?

DEATH AND POSSIBILITY

So, what we have to do is understand how we can be deprived of something, and be harmed by this deprivation, even if we are no longer around to be deprived of it. What this means, in effect, is that we are going to have to make sense of the idea that things can happen to us even when we are no longer around for them to happen to us. In other words, we are going to have to makes sense of the idea that much of what happens to us does not take place within the boundaries of our lives. If we can do this, then we will be, finally, getting somewhere. Can we make sense of this?

Here's one way of going about it, an approach based on the

notion of our *possibilities*. The idea is that we can suffer harm, even if we are no longer around when the harm takes place, because of possibilities that thereby go unrealised. That is, death harms us because it prevents the realisation of some of our possibilities. Death is harmful to the person who dies because it deprives that person of his or her possibilities. Will this idea work?

I don't think so. I don't think that possibilities are the right thing to be working with. The thing about possibilities is that they are, as we might say, *promiscuous*. Take Roy's death. This death is, at least for Roy, rather unfortunate. But this is not because the possibility that Roy becomes a flower arranger thereby goes unrealised. This is, in some sense, a possibility, but it is, I think, irrelevant to understanding why his death is harmful to Roy. Roy, I think we can safely infer from the general gist of the film, has no interest in being a flower arranger. And, surely, death cannot harm us by depriving us of possibilities in which we are in no way interested?

This is an illustration of the promiscuity of possibilities: there are far too many possibilities, and so there is nothing in a possibility that makes it intrinsically Roy's (or mine or yours). It is this promiscuity that lies at the heart of the problem. The original problem – the one that the appeal to possibilities was meant to solve – was the problem of how a person could be connected to events, like death, that lie outside of the temporal limits of that person's life, so that the person could be said to undergo those events. That is, the problem was of finding a way of *binding* that person to those events, so that those events could genuinely be said to happen to that person. We need to do this if we are to explain how death can harm us even if, when it happens, we are no longer around to be harmed. But appeal to possibilities merely replaces this problem with one of explaining what binds a person to his or her possibilities. We haven't got anywhere – we've merely exchanged one problem for another.

LOSING a FUTURE

This is where we're at. If death is a bad thing (for the person who dies), then this must be because it harms us. But if it harms us, then it must be because it is a harm of deprivation – it harms us because it deprives us of something. So, what sorts of things could death deprive us of, given that we are not around when it happens? Appealing to possibilities isn't going to work, since possibilities are too promiscuous to do the job required. Each one of us has far too many possibilities, and so there is nothing in any given possibility that makes it mine, as opposed to yours, or yours as opposed to mine. In short, we are not bound closely enough to our possibilities for deprivation of them to be a clear-cut case of harm. If we are to understand death as a harm of deprivation, then we must identify something to which we are more closely connected than mere possibilities. We have to understand death as depriving us of something we actually have, rather than merely possibly have.

One thing that death takes away from us is a *future*. Think about what goes into your life at any given moment. What this can be will vary from species to species and, within certain limits, from one human to another. For both humans and, it seems, replicants, what goes into one's life at any given time may be a constellation of experiences, beliefs, desires, goals, projects, activities and various other things. If you attend to the experiences, beliefs, desires, goals, projects and activities that you have at any given time – say now – then suppose that there is a time later than the present and, you are, or might be, having or undergoing the same sorts of things at this later time, then you understand the gist of what I mean by the future. That is, I use the term 'future' simply as shorthand for these sorts of things. When we die, we lose a future in this sense. This is why death harms us. Simple.

Or not. The sheen of simplicity is only apparent. The idea of losing a future is, when you think about it, a very strange one. And its strangeness comes from the strangeness of the idea of the future. The future does not yet exist. So how can you lose it? Indeed, you can lose a future only if you in some sense now have one. But how can you have something that does not yet exist? What this seems to show is that the ideas of *having* and *losing* in this context have a somewhat different meaning from when they occur in other, more usual, contexts. It is possible to have a future, but not in the same sense in which one might have broad shoulders or a Rolex watch. And if a renegade replicant were to deprive you of your future, the sense of the sense of deprivation would be quite different from when age deprives you of your shoulders, or a mugger deprives you of your watch.

In what sense, then, do we *have* a future? The danger is, of course, that the future is, itself, nothing more than a mere possibility. If so, we will be back with the idea that death harms us by depriving us of our possibilities. And this idea, as we have seen, is not going to work. So what we need is a way of understanding the future that makes it more than a mere possibility. Possibilities are things we only possibly have. So, what we need is a way of understanding the future that makes it something we *actually* have, rather something we merely *possibly* have. And we have to actually have this future now – at this moment in time – even though it does not exist yet. Tough one, but let's try to make sense of it.

minimal futures

There are, in fact, at least three different ways in which something can be said to *have* a future. First, there is a *minimal* sense in which everything that exists has a future (as long as it is not instantaneously destroyed). This book – the physical object that you hold in your hands – has a future at least in one sense. This means, simply, that there are times later than the present and the book will exist at those times. Of course if you, mistakenly thinking that the book is in fact a load of old twaddle, decide to consign the book to the flames then the book will no longer have a future. Throwing it in the fire will cause it to lose a future: as the flames consume the last portion of it, there will be no time later than the present at which that individual book will exist. Clearly, everything has a future, and just about everything can lose a future in this sense. There is a way of using the word 'harm' according to which it makes sense to say that the book is harmed when you throw it in the fire. But clearly the harm is very different in this case from the harm suffered when someone's life is taken away. This is, I shall argue, because the sense of deprivation is also very different in the two cases.

In this sense, having a future probably does amount to nothing more than a possibility. That there are times later than the present is, of course, highly likely, but not certain. Therefore, the future in this sense seems to be a possibility that has a high degree of probability of becoming actual. And, crucially, there is nothing in what you are doing in the present that connects you to the future in this sense. If we are to understand the harm of death in terms of the idea of losing a future, we need to look for more robust ways in which we might have, and so can lose, a future.

Being-towards-a-future

If we want to understand what's so bad about dying, we need to look at other, more substantial, ways in which something can have a future. But we also need to make the future something that we can *actually* have in the present – even though it doesn't yet exist – otherwise death wouldn't deprive us of it. How can we do this?

Here's a start. There are certain types of mental state that are, as we might say, *future-directed*. These mental states are ones that we actually possess now, at the present time. And so the idea is that you can have a future because you actually have now, at the present time, certain states that, in some sense, direct you towards times later than the present. The paradigmatic examples of such states would be *desires*, *goals* and *projects*.

In what sense is a desire future-directed? Well, here's one. Desires can be *satisfied* or *thwarted*. My desire for a beer will be satisfied if I walk to the refrigerator and get one. It will be thwarted if, for example, I open the refrigerator door and find the shelves bare. Roy's desire to kill the passengers and crew on the shuttle he is hijacking will be satisfied if he succeeds in doing so, thwarted if he does not.

The thing about desires is that satisfying them, typically, takes time. It takes time to walk to the refrigerator and open myself a bottle. It takes time to walk around a space shuttle blowing away all the humans on board. And this is *one* sense in which desires are future-directed: satisfying them takes time. The same is even more obviously true for goals and projects, both of which are, in all essentials, longer-term desires. My project of training six days a week takes time, as does my goal of becoming an Olympic triathlete. (Or, at least, these things would take time if I actually did or had them.) Roy's project of hijacking a space shuttle, travelling to Earth, kidnapping Eldon Tyrell and forcing him to remove the device that limits his lifespan takes time. Desires can be satisfied or thwarted, and goals and projects can be fulfilled or unfulfilled. And satisfying and fulfilling take time.

Therefore, I now, at the present time, have states that, in a reasonably clear sense, *direct me towards the future.* So does Roy. We all do. This is not to say that all desires are necessarily future-directed. You might, for example, desire that the past be other than it was (or is, depending on your view of the past). Nevertheless, many desires, almost certainly the vast majority, are future-directed in that their satisfaction takes time. Since the future does not yet exist, the only way you can have a future, in any genuine sense, is if you now, in the present, have states that direct you towards a future. These states exist, actually and now, even if the future they direct you towards does not. These presently existing states are future-directed: they relate you to your future and thus allow you, in a metaphorical but perfectly meaningful sense, to *have* that future. Therefore, as a first approximation, we can say that a person has a future, in a non-minimal sense, if he or she possesses certain future-directed states.

Because we now have actual states that direct us towards a future that does not yet exist, each one of us is, as the philosopher Martin Heidegger put it, *being-towards-a-future*. Each one of us, in our essential nature, is directed towards a future that does not yet exist. And in this sense at least, we can be said to have a future.

However, this is only a first approximation, and glosses over a crucial distinction, a distinction between two types of future-directed state. A state can be future-directed in two different ways. On the one hand, it may be a state that involves, as part of its content, a *concept* of the future. We can call such a state a *conceptually future-directed state*. On the other hand, a state can be directed towards the future in that although it contains, as part of its content, no concept of the future, the state does, nonetheless, require for its satisfaction that the person who has it persists beyond the present moment. I shall call this a *non-conceptually future-directed state*. The two types of state direct us towards a future in very different ways. And this difference is, I think, important to understanding why death is harmful.

CONCEPTS OF THE FUTURE

There is a big difference between the following two situations, and in the kinds of mental state involved.

Situation 1

Roy desires to blow away the passengers and crew on board a space shuttle. To satisfy this desire, he must walk around the shuttle, locate the passengers and crew, and shoot. So, Roy's desire is future-directed in that, in order for it to be satisfied, he must persist for at least a few moments into the future – as long as it takes for him to accomplish the necessary steps. The desire, in this sense, directs or binds Roy towards a future.

Situation 2

Pris asks Roy to list his plans for the future, after he has got Tyrell to remove the lifespan inhibitor. What he hopes to get out of life, where he hopes to be in twenty years' time and so on. In order to satisfy or fulfil his plans and goals, Roy, of course, needs to persist into the future. So, his plans and goals are future-directed in this sense. But, in this case, there also seems to be something more in the way in which they direct him into the future. For, in this case, it is explicitly recognised by Roy that the plans and goals he has are things 'for the future'. He recognises, that is, that they are things that cannot be satisfied now, but to which his present behaviour and actions can help make a contribution. Similarly, Roy wants to meet his maker, and thereby acquire more life. That is why he is, now, hijacking a shuttle and attempting the hazardous return to Earth. He recognises that his present efforts are directed at something – the removal of his lifespan inhibitor – that cannot happen now but might, if he is clever, careful and lucky, happen in the future.

The second situation, but not the first, involves a *concept* of the future. Roy's desire to kill the passengers and crew is future-directed in the sense that its satisfaction requires that he persist into the future as long as it takes to kill them. But Roy's having this desire does not require that he think, or even be able to think, to himself, 'My killing the humans on this shuttle, which will satisfy my desire, is an event that will take place in the future.' In order to have and satisfy this desire, by itself, Roy need have no concept of the future. The desire is one that *involves* the future, and does so quite centrally – because satisfying it takes time. But it does not involve, and having it does not require, a *concept* of the future.

However, in the second type of situation, it is explicitly recognised by Roy that his present desires and actions (e.g. the desire to kill the passengers and crew on the shuttle, and the effort he puts into satisfying this desire) are desires and actions that are directed towards further goals, ones that cannot be satisfied now but only in the future. So, in the second situation, Roy must be able to think explicitly about, or represent, the future. Desires that Roy has and things that Roy does in the second situation presuppose, and only make sense in terms of, a concept of the future.

The upshot of all this is that there are two different ways in which a mental state, such as a desire, goal or project, can direct you towards the future. There is, as in the case of Roy's desire to kill the humans on the shuttle, what we can call a *non-conceptual* way, one that does not involve an explicit concept of the future. Secondly, there is, as in the case of Roy's desire to get Tyrell to remove his lifespan limitation device, a *conceptual* way, one that does involve an explicit concept of the future. So, to mark this distinction, I am going to talk about mental states that are *conceptually future-directed*, or conceptually directed towards the future, and mental states that are *non-conceptually future-directed*, or non-conceptually directed towards the future.

WEAK AND STRONG FUTURES

Given that there are these two different ways – conceptual and non-conceptual – in which a state can be directed towards a future, there are also two different ways in which an individual – like you, me or Roy – can have a future. Someone will have a future in a *non-conceptual sense* if he, she or it has mental states that are non-conceptually future-directed. But someone will have a future in a conceptual sense if he, she or it has mental states that are conceptually future-directed. Each one of us is, as Heidegger put it, *being-towards-a-future*. But we can be this in two ways – non-conceptual and conceptual.

There is, I think, an intuitive sense in which someone who has a future in a conceptual sense is more closely, or intimately, bound to their future than someone who has a future in only a non-conceptual sense. Is this anything more than an intuition, or can we back it up with argument?

I think, to a considerable extent, that we can. A person who has a future in a conceptual sense is far more able to orient and organise his or her present behaviour and discipline and direct his or her present desires to achieve a desired future state than someone who does not. It is only because Roy has an explicit concept of the future – a future in which his lifespan inhibitor has been removed – that he can now, in the present, direct all his energies into getting into the same room as Eldon Tyrell. Because he is directing all his energies towards a goal that cannot be achieved now, but only in the future, Roy is investing much of his present time and energy in this future goal, and this invest-ment is possible only because he has an explicit concept of the future. The greater strength of Roy's connection to the future is, therefore, explained in terms of the greater disciplining, orient-ing and regimenting of his present behaviour, desires and other mental states. And this greater disciplining, orienting and regi-menting is made possible by the fact that he possesses a concept of the future and, on the basis of this, a desire that the future be a certain way.

Most of us, at least to some extent, have a tendency to 'live for tomorrow'. Much of what we do in the present we do not do for the sake of the present but for the future. After all, this is what becoming educated, building a career, remaining faithful to one's partner despite temptation, watching one's weight, taking out life insurance, are all about. But even simple mundane decisions, often so trivial as to be barely noticeable, are often infected by the future. No, I won't have one more drink, or I'll suffer tomorrow. No, I won't have that Twinkie, it'll ruin my appetite. For some of us, our orientation towards the future borders on the neurotic. But even for allegedly normal people, much of what we do in the present, perhaps the vast majority of what we do, only makes sense on the basis not only of the future but, more importantly, of our *concept* of the future.

An individual like Roy who has a concept of the future, and on the basis of this is conceptually directed towards his future, has more invested in that future than someone whose connection with the future is only non-conceptual. He is explicitly orienting and organising his present behaviour, and disciplining and direct-ing his present desires, on the basis of a conception of how he would like his future to be. Without a concept of the future, this cannot be done. Therefore, for this reason, I'll use the following terminology. An individual who has a future in a non-conceptual sense I shall say has a future in a *weak* sense. But an individual who has a future in a conceptual sense has, I shall say, a future in a *strong* sense. The difference between strong and weak posses-sion of a future, therefore, ultimately reflects a difference in the amount a person has *invested* in that future.

The relation between the two is something like this. If you have a future in the strong sense, then you automatically have one in a weak sense too. Having a future in a strong sense entails having one in a weak sense. Roy, with his explicit concept of a future, and the orienting of his present behaviour and his disciplining of his present desires that this concept makes possible, has a future in a strong sense (and therefore in a weak sense too). However, it is possible to have a future in a weak sense without having a future in a strong sense. This will happen if you are the sort of thing that can have desires without an explicit concept of the future. Satisfying your desires takes time, and this fact binds you to the future. But you don't have the explicit concept of the future that could allow you to orient your present behaviour and discipline your present desires in a way that would bind you to the future in any stronger sense.

LOSING A FUTURE AND
THE HARM OF DYING

Death is a bad thing because it deprives us of a future. Now, however, we see that it is possible to have a future in two different ways, a weak and a strong. Does this make a difference to the harm or badness of dying? Is dying worse for someone who has a future in a strong sense than for someone who has a future only in a weak sense?

I think it is. Someone who has a future in a strong sense, orienting much of their present behaviour, and disciplining many of their present desires, towards a conception of how they would like their future to be, is more closely tied, or bound, to their future than an individual who has a future in only a weak sense. Therefore, a person who has a future in a strong sense has more to lose, in losing a future, than a person who possesses a future in only a weak sense.

If this is not already clear, consider the following analogy. Two people get to the Olympics to compete in the triathlon. One has trained for years, oriented her life, organised her behaviour and disciplined her desires to achieve this goal. The other is a lazy, shiftless athlete who has reached the Olympics through, let us suppose, mistaken identity. Neither wins a medal. We sometimes talk of a person 'losing out' on the medals. If this is indeed a loss, then it seems that the greater loss is suffered by the first athlete, since she has organised her life around achieving this goal. Much of her life was lived for the sake of a future goal, which she did not achieve. She had, in a clear sense, more invested in getting a medal than did the other athlete. Therefore, her loss is greater.

I am basically making a similar point about the harm involved in losing a future. The more you have invested in the future, judged in terms of the organisation, orientation, disciplining and regimentation of your present behaviour and desires, then the more you lose when you lose that future. If you have a future in a conceptual, or strong sense, then, when you die, you lose more than if you had a future in only a weak, non-conceptual, sense. Death is a greater harm for those who have a future in a strong sense, for in dying they lose more than those who have a future in only a weak sense.

DEATH AND THE MEANING OF LIFE

So, we have worked out why death is a bad thing for the person who dies. We have worked out, that is, why death harms us. Death harms us because it takes away a future. But we have a future only because each one of us is *being-towards-a-future*. Each one of us, in our essence, is a being who is directed towards the future. This, and only this, is why death can harm us when we are no longer around to be harmed.

However, it seems reasonable to suppose that the harm of death is a function of the value that it takes away. If death harms us, then this must be because it takes away something of value. And this, it seems, will be the value of life. Death takes away the future, and we have a future because, and only because, we are *being-towards-a-future*. So it seems the value of life is intimately bound up with the fact that we are *being-towards-a-future*. And if the value of life is bound up with this, so too, it seems, is the meaning of life. But in what way?

We started off with the idea that death is the limit of a life, and so not an event in life, as the limit of a visual field is not something in that field. But we can make the same sort of point about each moment in life. Suppose we divide a person's life up into an arbitrary sequence of time-slices. It doesn't matter how long these are, but we will call each time-slice a *moment*. So, instead of considering a life as a whole, consider each moment in a person's life, however long that might be. Now, consider what happens when one moment passes over into the next. At the transition point, we have the limit – the end of the previous moment and the beginning of the next. But, as a limit, this transition point is not part of either moment. If it was, then it could not be the limit of each moment. A limit cannot be part of that which it limits. The death of each moment of a person's life is not part of that moment.

In these terms, to say that we are *being-towards-a-future* is to say that at each moment we are connected to future moments – even though they do not yet exist – because of the way we are in the original moment. This is what makes these future moments *ours*, and this is what makes these future moments that are ours succeed each other in a linear way. This is what makes the birth of one moment the death of the moment that preceded it. Our idea of a linear time derives from the sense we have that the birth of something that is mine is simultaneously the death of something that is also mine. And this sense of linearity is the key.

With the sense that the birth of something mine is also the death of something mine we also get the notion of *exclusion*. The satisfaction of one desire, goal or plan rules out the satisfaction of another. Why? Because time is linear. And as *being-towards-a-*

future we understand ourselves in terms of the ways we can be in that future. Satisfying one desire at the expense of another, following up on one plan while ignoring an alternative, this is what is involved in giving style to one's existence. This is what is involved in becoming what you are.

But you can become what you are only because other things are lost. You can become something – and so *be* something – only because following up on one possibility necessarily excludes others. There can be such a thing as *a* way of being only if one way of being automatically excludes other ways of being. Without this, we are no way at all. We are, so to speak, a *shapeless ontological mass.*

Time, specifically the linearity of time, is what permits one possible way of being to exclude others. One possible way of being can exclude others only because one moment excludes others. And one moment excludes others because we are *being-towards-a-future*. If we were not *being-towards-a-future*, we could not be anything at all.

So being anything at all requires linear time, and linear time requires the birth of one moment to be the death of the one that preceded it. The transition between moments is the limit or *horizon* that makes possible such a thing as a way of being. And the ultimate limit, the ultimate horizon, is death.

Consider, for example, what is required for a visual field to be a visual field? What would a visual field, for example, be like if it had no limit? This is almost certainly impossible to imagine. In a visual field, things (usually) make sense. And what is required in order for a visual field to make sense? Well, visual fields are structured or ordered spatially. Look around you: the table appears to the left of and slightly below the window, and to the right of the lampshade. Spatial ordering of this sort only makes sense relative to a frame of reference – some fixed point relative to which things can be ordered. Such a frame of reference requires a limit. Usually, for example, we order things in a visual field from the centre of that field – the table is slightly left of centre, the lampshade more so. But a visual field without a limit is, necessarily, a visual field without a centre. Without a limit, the visual field would have no structure, no order. It would not make sense.

Time is what gives structure and order to each one of us – it is what makes it possible for us to be what we are. Without it, we would not make sense. Time does not bring space into existence, but it is a precondition of the possibility of things in space having significance. Consider Roy's death soliloquy. What is the significance of that? If he had said it at any other point in his life, it would have had a quite different significance. For example, the speech would probably have appeared as quite comical if Roy had delivered it and then promptly recovered. And if he had said it when the possibility of death was not even on the horizon, then we probably would have figured he was just being neurotic, and told him to blow it out of his ass. Or we would have told him this if he wasn't a dangerously unhinged killer replicant.

The point is that the significance of an event in a life depends on *when* it occurs in that life. But without a temporal limit to life, nothing can have a temporal position in life. No more than something could have a spatial position in a limitless visual field. A visual field without a spatial limit is not a visual field at all. And a life without a temporal limit is, ultimately, not a life at all. The limit of a life is the *horizon* that permits individual events in that life to stand out as the things they are. And without this horizon, there is, in all essentials, nothing that means anything at all. Everything is a shapeless, hence senseless, ontological mass. Time, the passage of one moment to the next, is the horizon that allows us to be what we are. We are essentially *being-towards-a-future*. But death is the ultimate horizon against which the things in our life that make us what we are stand out. We are *being-toward-a-future*, but we are also, even more fundamentally, *being-towards-death*.

Death, as the horizon that allows us to stand out from being as a whole, is what gives our life meaning. Death may be that which takes away our life, and so takes away whatever value that life had for us. But it is also that which gives meaning to life in the first place. The source of the harm of death and the value of life is the same, and it is this: we are essentially *beings-towards-death*. When we die, all these moments will indeed be lost in time, like tears in rain. But that these moments were found at all, indeed existed at all, is only because we are death-bound beings. Time to die.

GLOSSARY

Absurdity Arguably a central feature of human existence, and figures prominently in the philosophical movement known as **existentialism**. Absurdity is engendered by a clash between the view we have of ourselves from the inside and the view that exists from the outside. This clash is also symptomatic of deep philosophical problems. So, absurdity can be claimed to lie at the core of philosophy as well as human existence.

Agent causation theory A view concerning the philosophical issue of human freedom. According to agent causation theory, human actions are free when, and only when, they are brought about by the self or person. Problems for agent causation theory include making sense of the notion of **self** that supposedly brings about these actions, and understanding just how it is supposed to bring them about.

Aristotle Greek philosopher, and maybe the best ever. Studied under Plato at his school, The Academy, in Athens, and, in turn, went on to tutor Alexander the Great. He made significant contributions to just about every area of philosophy, including **metaphysics**, **ethics** and politics. His influence declined after the Renaissance and scientific revolution of the seventeenth century, but still the official philosopher of the wonderfully reactionary Catholic Church.

Berkeley, George Eighteenth-century Irish philosopher and bishop. Defender of a version of **idealism**. Reality is ultimately mental, a collection of ideas in the mind of God. When you look at the world around you, God flashes the appropriate ideas into your mind. And He does the same for everyone. God, trying to hold everything together in Berkeley's idealist scheme of things, is about as busy as a one-legged man in an ass-kicking contest.

Body theory The view that the identity of a person is determined by their body. The essential core of the person is the body, the whole body, and nothing but the body. The view was essentially refuted by Arnie in *Total Recall*, when he showed that two persons – Quaid and Hauser – could both have occupied the same body at different times.

Brain in a vat Imaginative device used to motivate **scepticism** about the external world. If you are a brain in a vat, being electrically stimulated by appropriately skilled scientists, you might not be able to tell you are a brain in a vat. If so, you cannot be certain that you are not a brain in a vat. Therefore, you can't be certain that you have a body. Therefore, you cannot be certain that what you think of as the real world is real at all. A variation on this theme provided the intellectual underpinning for *The Matrix*, and it is a modern-day counterpart to **Descartes's** thought experiments.

Brain theory The view that the identity of a person is determined by their brain. The essential core of any person is their brain, and wherever there is the same (functioning) brain there is the same person.

Camus, Albert Twentieth-century French existentialist philosopher and friend of Sartre. Camus was the only existentialist who didn't explicitly deny being an existentialist. Wrote lots of books about alienation, outsiders and the futility of human existence. Thought that not committing suicide was an act of great heroism. Miserable sod.

Categorical imperative Immanuel **Kant's** fundamental rule of morality: 'I ought never to act except in such a way that I can also will that my maxim should become a universal law.' This ties morality closely to consistency. Morally good actions must be ones that can be consistently adopted by everyone. Probably a jargonised version of the golden rule: do unto others ...

Cogito, ergo sum Latin, 'I think, therefore I am.' Probably the most famous philosophical claim ever, and made by **Descartes**. It is used to express the idea that it is not possible to doubt your own existence because you would have to exist in order to do the doubting.

Compatibilism The view that human freedom is perfectly compatible with causation. **Hume** was a famous compatibilist. The freedom of an action consists in its being caused *in the right way*, namely by your wants or desires. You are, in other words, free if you can do as you please. Susceptible to the objection that in order to be really free you have to be able to please as you please and not just do as you please.

Consciousness Can mean at least 27 different things. In philosophy it is often used to refer to the way it seems or feels to have an experience. For example, you stub your toe, and it hurts. This way it feels is an example of *phenomenal* consciousness. Psychologists use the term in a completely different way, and the mutual misunderstandings this engenders contributes to the contempt that each holds for the other.

Consequentialism The view that the rightness or wrongness of an action is determined by, and only by, the consequences of that action. Nothing else counts. In particular, the motives or intentions that you have for doing something count for nothing. The saying that the road to hell is paved with good intentions was coined by a consequentialist. Consequentialist views are opposed to **deontological** views of morality.

Deontological A moral theory is deontological if it claims that the rightness or wrongness of an action is determined, at least in part, by the motive, intention or *maxim* that the agent has for performing the action. That's not the whole story; consequences count too. But motives and intentions count for at least something. Opposed to **consequentialism**.

Descartes, René Seventeenth-century French philosopher, scientist, mathematician and mercenary. Often called the 'father of modern philosophy'. Also one of the principal architects of **dualism**. He was wrong on just about everything, but due to one of the many perversions of justice that have scarred the history of philosophy is still regarded as one of the greats. Lazy bastard who liked to sleep until at least lunchtime. Died after getting a job that required him to get up at 5.00 a.m.

Determinism The view that everything that exists or occurs has a cause, and therefore humans are not free. The connection is that causes make their effects inevitable, and so human actions, choices and decisions, being inevitable, cannot be free. Difficult view to refute. Spielberg and Cruise tried their best in *Minority Report*, but their treatment was, I think, inadequate.

Dualism The theory that the mind is a non-physical thing of some sort, and that humans are made up of a physical body coupled with a non-physical mind. One of the most refuted views in all of philosophy, though that hasn't stopped some people believing it. Strongly associated with **Descartes**.

Egoism The view that you should act to further your own interests, whatever they may be. Kevin Bacon did his best to defend a form of egoism in *Hollow Man*. There are stupid egoists and there are rational egoists. The main difference is that rational egoists are a lot more sneaky, and while they may be doing things that seem, on the face of it, to be nice or considerate, are really just lulling you into a false sense of security while they hatch their clever plan to screw you over. Most academics are rational egoists.

Empiricism The view that all our knowledge comes from experience. Actually, not all our knowledge. You don't need to look around the world to find out that there are no married bachelors, for example. You can know this from the meanings of the words involved. This is sometimes called trivial knowledge. Empiricism is the view that all our non-trivial knowledge must come from experience. **Berkeley** and **Hume** were empiricists.

Epicurus Greek philosopher of fourth and third centuries BC, and one of the most misunderstood ever. Commonly thought of as a party dude, a rampant **hedonist** who valued the pursuit of pleasure above all other things. In fact he advocated the moderation of one's desires as the true path to happiness. Famous for claiming that death cannot harm us.

Epistemology The study of knowledge and how much of it we can have. From Greek *episteme* (knowledge) and *logos* (logic). Famous epistemological themes were developed by

Plato and **Descartes**. Epistemology has nothing to do with skiing or drunkenness.

Ethics The branch of philosophy that deals with the nature of right and wrong. Philosophers have always thought that they had the corner of this market, ever since **Plato** connected up reality and goodness in his **theory of forms**. If goodness and reality are one and the same, the study of reality is the study of goodness. It is arguable that this was simply a confidence trick of breathtaking brilliance, aimed at getting people to pay to attend his school in fourth-century BC Athens. Between you and me, if I wanted to find out about right and wrong, the last person I would ask is a philosopher.

Evil demon One of the imaginative devices used by **Descartes** to show that we cannot be certain that the external world exists. It is possible that the universe is controlled by an evil demon that gets his/her/its kicks from constantly deceiving us. Most scholars think that Descartes's thoughts on this subject incontrovertibly prove the existence of crack cocaine in seventeenth-century France.

Existentialism A twentieth-century philosophical movement, headed by figures such as **Heidegger** and **Sartre**. The basic idea is that human beings, not being created by God, have no nature, and therefore are condemned to be free. In fact, the only thing we are not free to be is not free. To deny this freedom is to be *inauthentic* or in *bad faith*. The curious thing about existentialists is that no one really wanted to own up to being one (thereby, one might think, engaging in a little bad faith of their own). Heidegger vociferously denied it all of his life, even though his employment of central existentialist concepts, such as *authenticity*, *anxiety* and *being-towards-death* clearly marked him out as one. Sartre wrote a famous paper entitled 'Existentialism is a humanism', which was pretty much a dead give-away as to his affiliations. However, he later became a Marxist, wrote *Critique of Dialectical Reason*, and claimed that he could not believe he had held his earlier views. **Camus** was about the only existentialist who was consistently happy being called an existentialist.

Facticity Existentialist term for those features of you or your situation over which you have little or no control. For example, you are an ugly geek, with a laughably small penis and an IQ of 73. Too bad, mate, it's your facticity. Facticity can also mean features of your situation rather than yourself. You wake one morning, and lying next to you is the most stunningly unprepossessing member of the opposite sex you could ever imagine (well, of course it is, you're an ugly geek with a small penis, who did you expect, Giselle?). Too bad, again, mate – it's your facticity. Facticity is not unremittingly negative. You wake up and it *is* Giselle, because you are Leonardo DiCaprio just after you starred in *Titanic*. Facticity too.

Fission, problem of An objection to the **memory theory** of personal identity. If a clone of you is made, your original body destroyed, and your memories transferred to the clone, then, by the memory theory, you should survive as your clone. However, if, by accident, two clones are somehow made, and your memories transferred to both, then the memory theory has a problem. You can't be both resulting people, but neither can you be one rather than the other. But this can't mean that you don't survive the procedure – a double success does not add up to a failure. The problem was originally developed by the Oxford philosopher Derek Parfit. Its most convincing defence has probably been given by Arnie in *The Sixth Day*.

Forms, theory of Metaphysical theory developed by **Plato**. Ultimate reality consists in a non-physical realm of forms – perfect examples of things. The most perfect of the forms was the form of the good: perfect goodness. You could have knowledge of the form of the good only if you were suitably trained – i.e. by Plato.

Gyges Legendary founder of line of kings of Lydia. Reputed to possess a ring of invisibility, which he used to ends that can alternately be judged as nefarious or ingenious, depending on whether you are talking to **Kant** or a **social contract** theorist. There is no firm evidence that he was inordinately fond of sheep.

Hedonism The view that pleasure is the ultimate **intrinsic** human good. Contrary to what we are told by most religions, seeking pleasure is not wrong. It is, in fact, the ultimate ethical goal of life.

Heidegger, Martin Twentieth-century German philosopher. Always on the make. Basically endorsed Hitler and Nazism in an infamous speech in 1933, and was immediately appointed Rector of the University of Freiburg; a coincidence I'm sure. Total bastard. On the other hand, was a rather good philosopher. His most famous work was *Being and Time*.

Heraclitus Greek philosopher of fifth-century BC. Most famous claim was that you can't step into the same river twice. Insane, but mostly harmless.

Hobbes, Thomas Seventeenth-century English philosopher. Defended a **social contract** view of morality and used it to argue for a form of monarchy in which absolute power would be lodged in an authority that he termed the *Leviathan*. This was also the title of his most famous work. Bit of a fascist really, and probably would have been a big admirer of Saddam Hussein.

Hume, David Eighteenth-century Scottish philosopher and all-round regular good guy. Prominent defender of **empiricism**, but said lots of interesting stuff about lots of different things.

Idealism The view that reality is ultimately mental, a collection of ideas in someone or other's mind. **Berkeley** defended a form of idealism that had God doing most of the work: reality was a collection of ideas in the mind of God, which he kindly flashed into the minds of humans at appropriate junctures. **Kant** also defended a form of idealism, a less extreme form which he called *transcendental idealism*. Reality exists independently of our ideas, but we can know nothing about it. This he called *noumenal* reality and distinguished it from the *phenomenal* reality that we perceive, know and understand.

Identity, numerical Literal identity. You are numerically identical with you, and you alone, and not, for example, with your evil twin brother (or sister) Skippy even though he/she is virtually indistinguishable from you. Similarly, Adam Gibson, in *The Sixth Day*, is numerically identical only with Adam Gibson, and not with his clone.

Identity, qualitative Close or exact similarity. You are qualitatively identical with your evil twin brother Skippy because you exactly resemble each other. Adam Gibson is qualitatively identical with his twin, even though they are, numerically, different people.

Incompatibilism The view that freedom and causation are incompatible. If our actions, choices and decisions are caused, then, according to incompatibilism, they cannot be free. **Determinism** is a form of incompatibilism. So too is **Indeterminism**.

Indeterminism The view that at least some human actions, choices and decisions do not have causes and that they are, therefore, free. It is precisely because they do not have causes that they are free. The main objection to indeterminism is that it confuses freedom with randomness of spontaneity.

Instrumental value Value that a thing has because of some other thing that it can help you get. Money and medicine, for example, are valuable not for what they are in themselves but for other things they can get you.

Intentionality The aboutness or directedness of (some) mental states. The belief that Keanu Reeves is the star of *The Matrix* is a belief about Keanu Reeves. The belief is, in some way, directed towards Keanu, and because of this is about him. This directedness or aboutness is what philosophers mean when they talk about intentionality. There are lots of problems trying to understand precisely what this relation of aboutness is and, arguably, no one has yet come up with a satisfactory theory of it.

Intrinsic value Value that a thing has independently of anything else. According to hedonists, pleasure is intrinsically valuable because you want it for its own sake and not for other things that it can get you. According to Nietzsche, on the other hand, power is intrinsically valuable. Sometimes called *inherent* value.

Kant, Immanuel Eightheenth-century German philosopher. Most influential philosopher of the past 200 years. Made significant contributions to **metaphysics**, **epistemology** and **ethics**. Led a very uneventful life, and therefore difficult to take the piss out of. Did have a big nose though.

Laplace's demon Hypothetical super-being capable of exactly predicting the future state of the universe based on a complete and exhaustive knowledge of its present state. Imagine the precogs of *Minority Report*, and then imagine their powers extended to cover not just murders but everything else too. Then you'll have a pretty good idea of what Laplace's demon can do.

Materialism The view that reality is ultimately physical or material in nature. In connection with the **mind–body problem**, it is the view that the mind is a physical thing, typically the brain. The position defended by Arnie in *Terminator* (I and II).

Memory theory The view that the identity of a person is determined by their memories and other psychological states. The essential core of a person consists in a network of related psychological states. This was the view so vividly defended by Verhoeven–Schwarzenegger in *Total Recall* (before Arnie went on to reconsider his commitment to this view in *The Sixth Day*).

Metaphysics The branch of philosophy that deals with the nature of reality. More or less the same as **ontology**.

Mind–body problem The problem of explaining the nature of the mind and its relation to the body. Attempts to answer this problem can, broadly, be divided into two sorts: **dualism** and **materialism**.

Nietzsche, Friedrich Nineteenth-century German philosopher, associated with the idea of will to power and the superman. In reality Nietzsche was a total wimp who was probably beaten up at school, and who never really got over being dumped by Lou Salome. Syphilis, almost certainly contracted in a youthful indiscretion in a whorehouse, hastened his decline into madness.

Ontology The study of existence or the nature of reality. From Greek *onta* (things) and *logos* (logic).

Plato Greek philosopher of fifth and fourth century BC. Claimed that true reality consisted in a world of forms, and that it was possible to have knowledge of such a world, especially if you attended the school he set up, the **Academy**. According to Alfred North Whitehead, the history of Western philosophy is a series of footnotes to Plato, but Whitehead was largely insane. Plato was taught philosophy by Socrates and, as was the fashion at the time, probably buggered by him too.

Practical imperative Kant's reformulation of the categorical imperative: 'Act in such a way that you always treat humanity whether in your own person or in the person of any other, never simply as a means but always at the same time as an end.' Which is Kant's way of saying be nice and considerate to everyone. He really did need to get out more.

Predestination The view that what happens in the future is inevitable irrespective of what happens in the present. Despite a common tendency to confuse the two, this is quite different from **determinism**.

Sartre, Jean-Paul Twentieth-century French existentialist philosopher and literary figure. Active in the French resistance in the Second World War, or so he repeatedly keeps reminding us. Most famous work was *Being and Nothingness*. Possibly the ugliest philosopher who ever lived, but still a big hit with women (whom he generally treated very badly).

Scepticism The view that knowledge is not possible in some or other area of enquiry. For example, scepticism about the external world is the view that we cannot know whether this world exists and/or whether it is the way we think it is; scepticism about moral values is the view that we cannot know what's right and wrong, and so on.

Self The essential core of the person. That which persists through all the changes a person undergoes in the course of his life. It is possible that there is no such thing. At least that's one way of reading what Arnie was trying to show us in *The Sixth Day*.

Social contract The idea that the scope of morality can be understood in terms of the idea of a social contract – a hypothetical bargain that would be struck by rational individuals to regulate the interactions between them. The rules of morality reduce to the rules of this contract. Defended by **Hobbes**.

Socrates Extremely ugly Greek philosopher of the fifth century BC. He thought of himself as a 'gadfly' whose mission was to sting the intellectual conscience of his fellow Athenians. His fellow Athenians, on the other hand, thought of him as an annoying little shit, and tried to do away with him in various ways. After he was ungracious enough to survive the front line in the Peloponnesian War, they finally lost all patience and made him drink poison in 399 BC. Fond of buggering boys.

Soul theory The view that the identity of a person is determined by the presence, within their body, of a non-physical mind or soul. The core of any person is the soul, and, so, wherever there is the same soul there is the same person. Version of dualism.

Speciesism The view that members of species X have less moral standing than members of species Y, simply because they are not members of species Y. For example, the view that members of a non-human species have less moral standing than humans simply because they are not human.

Sub specie aeternitatis Latin, 'Beneath the gaze of eternity'. Corresponds to the idea of a perspective that is not limited by the partial, parochial or subjective interests of the perceiver.

Utilitarianism Moral theory associated with the eighteenth- and nineteenth-century English philosophers Jeremy Bentham and John Stuart Mill. Happiness is intrinsically good and, accordingly, morally good actions are ones that produce the greatest amount of happiness for the greatest number of people. Sometimes described as a form of social **hedonism**.

Volition An act of will, especially one preceding a bodily movement. The power of deciding, choosing or acting.

Wittgenstein, Ludwig Twentieth-century Austrian philosopher, who thought that philosophical problems exist because we have been led astray by language. Most famous works were *Tractatus Logico-Philosophicus* and (the posthumously published) *Philosophical Investigations*. The youngest member of an extremely rich and gifted family, many of whom were totally fucked up in one way or another and found interesting ways to kill themselves. Wittgenstein spent much of his adult life at Cambridge, except for a twelve-year period after the First World War, which he spent teaching in a village school in the middle of nowhere, Austria. Rumour has it that he was kicked out of the school for slapping the kids around when they refused to grasp the finer points of second-order predicate logic. Not a nice man.